AN
AFRICAN GIFT

AN
ÅFRICAN GIFT

My Life with the
Batwa Pygmies

Dr. Scott Kellermann

Surrogate Press®

Published in the United States by
Surrogate Press®
an imprint of Faceted Press®
Park City, Utah

Surrogate Press, LLC
SurrogatePress.com

ISBN: 978-1-964245-01-0
Library of Congress Control Number: 2024910406

Cover design by: Michelle Rayner, Cosmic Design LLC
Cover photo by: Peter Bauza
Interior design by: Katie Mullaly, Surrogate Press®

The publishing of *An African Gift* is lovingly donated by the Kellermann
Foundation Board of Directors in honor of Dr. Scott and Carol Kellermann
and in thanksgiving for their deep devotion to helping people in need.

"If you have much, give of your wealth;
if you have little, give of your heart."
—— • African Proverb • ——

All proceeds from this book are donated
to the Kellermann Foundation
Kellermannfoundation.org

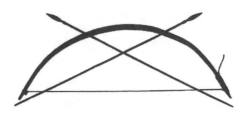

Table of Contents

Preface: In the Moment 1

Part I (2000 – 2001)
Discovering a Call

Chapter 1: The Beginning of a Change 6

Chapter 2: We Arrive 11

Chapter 3: The Plight of the Batwa 18

Chapter 4: Gorillas Flourishing, Humans Not.............. 34

Chapter 5: Learning to Listen................................ 42

Chapter 6: Finding our Voice 51

Chapter 7: Discovering the Source 57

Part II (2001 – 2003)
Mobile Medicine

Chapter 8: Medical Practice Under the Ficus Tree........ 64

Chapter 9: Essential Medicines 70

Chapter 10: Father Fred's Redemption 77

Chapter 11: An Injured Back and a Missing Key........... 83

Chapter 12: A Geography Lesson 88

Chapter 13: Springs of Living Water 94

Chapter 14: Being Faithful 98

Part III (2003 – 2010)
Hope

Chapter 15: New Hope....................................... 104

Chapter 16: Ant Attack 110

Chapter 17: Land and Health 116

Chapter 18: Discovering Abundance in Community 122

Chapter 19: Out of Stock 127

Chapter 20: A Thin Veil Between the Living and the Dead 132

Chapter 21: Visionary Friends 139

Chapter 22: Lessons in Generosity 143

Chapter 23: Insurance Plans 153

Part IV (2011 – 2017)
Partners in Health

Chapter 24: The Batwa Take Charge of Their Destiny 162

Chapter 25: Strong Women, Woven Together 175

Chapter 26: A Healing Partnership 179

Chapter 27: Malaria Struck Down, and Doctor Struck Out 187

Chapter 28: Partnering Against Tuberculosis 197

Chapter 29: HIV and Peace 203

Chapter 30: The Weighty Issues of Poverty and Education 209

Chapter 31: The Care of Mothers 216

Part V (2017 and Beyond)
For the Future

Chapter 32: From the Rainforest to the UN 224

Chapter 33: The Birth of a Nursing School 231

Chapter 34: Going Home 236

Acknowledgements 243

About the Author 246

PREFACE

✤ ✤ ✤

In the Moment

"God has created lands with lakes and rivers for man to live.
And the desert so that he can find his soul."

──✦ • Tuareg Proverb • ✦──

I awake in my tent after a good night's rest. I kiss my wife Carol and step outside. A thick mist blankets the ground. The air is redolent of wood smoke. I'm almost overwhelmed by the sounds of the jungle. The calls of bush-shrikes and hadada ibis, the shrieks of monkeys, and the deep grunts of colobus. While the sounds are more jarring than a morning alarm clock, they blend into a kind of music. What brings even greater pleasure is that, after a morning wash in a nearby stream, I'll continue my work providing medical outreach to Batwa (pronounced bä-Twä) pygmies.

I sit on a fallen log before dipping into the chilly water and reflect on what I have learned from the Batwa. The Batwa live in the moment; as hunter-gatherers, their language utilizes primarily the present tense. Even events occurring in the distant past are expressed in the present. This makes dwelling on the past and planning for the future difficult, but it's an interesting way to communicate and to live.

I understand how living in the present has its value, particularly when one is just trying to make it from one day to the next. But how does one consider hope?

Refreshed from the splash in the stream, I return to the tent. I say to Carol, "The Batwa speak primarily in the present tense. Despite their difficult life, they seem filled with hope; but isn't hope a future concept?"

After reflecting for a few moments, Carol notes with a smile, "Although I hope that we can find something to eat for breakfast, perhaps hope cannot be experienced except in the present."

Carol continues, "You remember the retreats we have attended that focused on mindfulness, where we were encouraged to live in the moment? Perhaps the Batwa will help us in this practice."

I find myself thinking, speaking, and living in the present tense. I've stopped wearing a watch. These memoirs are mostly written in the present tense, just as we experienced them. Of course, moments connect to form a story. The story I tell in this book of our years in Uganda and the precious gifts we have received from the Batwa and so many other Africans is a testament to God's gracious care; it is a hopeful story, full of moments of both struggle and joy. As I recall these moments, or gather them from my journals, I am filled with gratitude. I write them here with hope that others can share this gratitude with me.

In this moment, on the fifteenth day of June 2001, we have been camping outside of a Batwa village in southwest Uganda. There's no medical facility, not even a simple shed in which to treat my patients. I've set up a makeshift "clinic" under a nearby ficus tree, a tree that towers 150 feet above us. It provides both support for the IVs and shade for the patients.

I feel confident. I have my day pretty well mapped out, my medications at the ready, and patients are drifting in. But my plans are immediately shattered. A mother rushes up cradling her dying child.

The child is severely anemic due to malaria and desperately needs a transfusion. The nearest hospital is a long distance away. When I look around, almost a hundred expectant patients are staring at me. I see mothers holding their children, anxious for my care, while some rest patiently nearby.

Dr. Scott monitoring IVs under the ficus tree

A decision must be made: attempt to save the child or attend to the needs of the many others who have come for medical care. There are no easy answers this morning. No amount of medical training and no experience I have gained dealing with medical crises in the United States could prepare me for a decision like this. Carol, who has overheard the conversation, takes the child from me, turns to the mother and the crowd simply saying, "*Tu gendye!*" (Let's go).

We leave the patients in the care of a few locals whom we have trained in rudimentary medicine and pile into our beat-up ambulance, taking a one-hour drive to the government hospital. When we arrive, a nurse sadly informs us that IV supplies and blood are not available. "I am sorry that you came all this way." This child's life can only be saved by driving another hour and a half to a well-appointed Catholic facility. We do. I deliver the child into the care of a smiling nurse wearing a starched white cap and a neatly pressed uniform. Carol gives the mother money to pay for the hospital's services and we depart.

On the drive back, Carol voices her dream: "I hope one day we can have a clean medical facility staffed with trained personnel and supplied with the medicine needed to treat the Batwa." I agree, but I realize this is but a dream. We're in a remote area of Uganda. How could we ever build a hospital here?

When we return, after an absence of over six hours, the crowd has not dispersed. If anything, it has swelled. Our announcement that the child will live is greeted with singing and dancing. We get down to our work, treating patients, administering IV medications to the sickest, providing oral medications to others, and always dispensing hope. We don't quit until a bright yellow sun begins to drop behind the rugged hills.

PART I (2000 – 2001)
Discovering a Call

"If you want to know the end, look at the beginning."

— · African Proverb · —

CHAPTER 1

✢ ✢ ✢

The Beginning of a Change

*"When the rhythm of the drumbeat changes,
the dance step must adapt."*

——— • African Proverb • ———

It is the year 2000. For several decades, my wife Carol and I have been "living large," occupying a roomy house on a substantial plot of land outside of Nevada City, California. Carol carefully maintains an enormous garden. Her homegrown fruits and vegetables are the mainstays of our family during the summer and fall. We particularly enjoy winter, taking vacations in our mountain cabin in the Serene Lakes area of the Sierra Nevada Mountains.

"Life happens," as they say, "in our most unguarded moments." A record season of snowfall collapses the roof of our Sierra cabin. The repair bills are more spectacular than the snowfall. Not long after that, our children leave for college, our house is suddenly far too large, the ski cabin is collecting dust, the telephone rings infrequently, and the fridge is full. We realize that some middle-aged adjustments are needed.

As my nametag proclaims, I am "Scott Kellermann, M.D." and I have a very busy family medical practice in town. I am also chief-of-staff at Sierra Nevada Hospital, our local hospital, and serve on its board of directors. With two other physicians, I have purchased an aging hospital. Together, we have started an indigent care clinic that has grown to become the largest healthcare provider in Nevada County.

The bills for my malpractice insurance are enormous. I work long into the evenings. Freed from her child rearing routines, Carol has begun pursuing counseling training in San Francisco. Additionally, Carol and I have both become more active in our local Trinity Episcopal Church, which we find life giving. And yet, I realize that at age fifty-five, we are, for the most part, operating on cruise control; although, there is little time to think about making a change.

An awakening comes from a patient's initial visit to my office. I apologize to the patient as I attempt to navigate the recently installed, innovative-but-quirky, electronic medical record system. I ask this young, demure, well-dressed woman the litany of sequenced 'first medical visit' questions from the list on the computer.

"What is your date of birth?"

"Are you employed?"

"What medical problems have you had in the past?"

"Tell me the medical history of your family members."

"Please tell me about your husband and your children."

As she answers, I intently stare at the computer screen, clicking boxes and entering the data she provides.

When I inquire what brings her into the office, I happen to look up at her face. I am shocked to see tears tracking down her cheeks.

"What could possibly be the matter?" I ask.

She says, "My husband and I are having marital difficulties, but you seem too busy with the computer to care."

I haven't really been listening. I glance back to the cursor blinking over a blank box. Which am I? A computer that gathers information, or an agent of healing?

I have practiced medicine in harsh environments, particularly in Kathmandu where our youngest son, Josh, was born; I have worked in emergency rooms across the U.S. treating individuals in medical crises; and I have worked with medical missions in Brazil in the festering slums of Sao Paulo. These times come back to me as I ask myself about what I am really doing as a medical doctor. I recall the times when I felt challenged but also felt a deep connection and joy that comes from practicing a healing profession. I wonder if I should consider that kind of change to remember why I had become a doctor.

Moreover, Carol and I are both aware that change is needed in our relationship. There has been strength in our marriage, punctuated by the occasional squabble, but we are drifting apart, physically, emotionally, and spiritually. Our goals lack a common thread, and we are sharing less and planning fewer activities together.

One night, Carol comments, "We used to talk about our kids, but now that they are out of the house, we don't chat much." Like my patient, Carol complains, "You are spending too much time on the computer and not enough on me!"

Unbeknownst to me, five years earlier, in 1995, the Anglican archbishop of the Church of Uganda made a stop in Dallas, Texas. There, he approached Diane Stanton, the wife of the Bishop of the Episcopal Diocese of Dallas. As Diane later recounted the story, the archbishop was an impressive figure: tall, jet-black hair, and a gleaming smile. He wore a clerical collar, a purple shirt indicative of his office, and a well-worn suit. In a deeply resonant voice, he asked Diane, "Can you help me?" Assuming he wanted a glass of water or directions to the bathroom, Diane responded, "Yes, of course, what would you like?" To her amazement, he enquired, "I need your help in saving a tribe." Diane was riveted to the spot as he continued, "The Batwa tribe has been expelled from the Bwindi Impenetrable Forest and is in dire need of resettlement. Will you assist?" Diane thought to herself, "This request is for a bit more than a glass of water!" Collecting herself, she told the archbishop, "I will do what I can."

Faithful to her word, Diane pursued this strange request by contacting the Anglican bishop in Kanungu, Uganda, where the

Batwa were located. Based on the needs he described, Diane set about raising funds to buy land, build a school, and construct a clinic to address their critical health issues and immunize the community. However, without the electricity needed to refrigerate the vaccines, along with the long distances involved in delivering it to the villages, the immunization program stalled, the clinic faltered, and death rates continued to climb. The Batwa were vanishing. In hopes that these pressing medical problems could somehow be addressed, Diane reached out to the Houston-based Episcopal Medical Missions Foundation (EMMF) requesting medical oversight from the U.S. for the clinic and the Batwa resettlement.

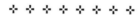

Back again to 2000 when I am wondering which way to turn, both in my marriage and medicine, I spot the EMMF internet posting requesting a physician who was willing to spend at least a month in Uganda with the Batwa. It captures my imagination. What great work! And in Africa, where so many of the diseases that fascinate me lurk.

Before turning in one night, I raise the possibility to Carol of responding to this need in Uganda. She listens attentively as I describe the plight of the Batwa, what this project would require of us, and how we might work together.

I conclude with, "Do you remember your response to my statement years ago, that Africa has the best diseases?"

How could we forget? Carol and I met when I was studying medicine at Tulane University. For me, meeting Carol was like a Hollywood story: spotting the most beautiful woman in the room and immediately thinking that I wanted to spend my life with her. Her intelligence and wit sealed the deal. We married in Los Angeles on November 29, 1975. After internship at the University of Southern California and residency at the University of California, LA, we returned to Tulane for a year of advanced surgical training. There, Carol gave birth to Seth, our first son.

Tulane has a School of Public Health and Tropical Medicine. When someone pointed me in that direction, I became fascinated with what I began to learn about: flesh-destroying tropical ulcers, dysentery, malaria, sleeping sickness, leprosy, schistosomiasis, and myriads of other bizarre and fascinating diseases that made anything I'd seen at LA County Hospital look timid. Moreover, these diseases afflict a large portion of the world's poor.

Here is the scene as we both remember it: Carol and I often read to each other before turning in at night. One night in 1976, as we lay with our infant son between us, rather inappropriately, I decided to read to her from *Manson's Book of Tropical Diseases*. Nothing like hearing about debilitating or fatal diseases before nodding off. Yet, I persisted, reading on to Carol about a disease called "Noma," meaning "to devour."

I read aloud, "Noma is a necrosis that develops from bacteria in the mouth, usually in poverty-stricken, West African adolescents. It will eat away the tissues of the face in a matter of weeks. It has an 80 to 90 percent mortality rate, and the few who survive have huge chunks of their faces destroyed, requiring major plastic surgery to repair the damage."

I pointed to some photos in the book. As Carol was trying to recover from the gruesome pictures, I said, "Sweetie, all the best diseases are in Africa. Let's go!" Diplomacy and finesse have never been my strong suits, but I have never lacked for energy. I thought that my enthusiasm would be contagious. It wasn't. Carol clutched our newborn to her chest and said emphatically, "You'll never get me to Africa!"

Yet today, while discussing the EMMF posting, when I remind Carol of that night and what she said, she simply smiles and says, "That was twenty years ago. I'm ready now. Let's get some sleep and we'll start planning tomorrow."

Within a week, we have two airline tickets to Uganda.

CHAPTER 2

✣ ✣ ✣

We Arrive

"If you don't know where you are going,
any road will take you there."

———— • Ugandan Proverb • ————

The Bwindi Impenetrable Forest is located in southwest Uganda in sub-Saharan Africa, an area sometimes referred to as "Darkest Africa." Henry Morgan Stanley, an explorer famous for his search for Dr. David Livingstone in Africa, first used that term in an account of one of his expeditions. The tag "darkest" labeled the continent for its lack of modern influences and resistance to colonization. The term is at once condescending and racist. Stanley's book describes people who live in the "jungle" as not only uneducated but virtually subhuman.

As we began to interact with the Batwa, their joy in the midst of great adversity taught us more about humanity than half a century of living and practicing medicine in the West. The Batwa are a hardy people who have lived in the Bwindi Forest for thousands of years. Using bows and poison-tipped arrows or nets, the men hunted small game such as bush pigs, duikers (small antelopes), and birds. The women gathered various plants and fruits that are abundant in the Bwindi. Small, temporary huts, constructed with leaves and branches, were abandoned after a few months when the Batwa relocated to other parts of the forest in search of more food. Their tools were primitive, pre-Stone Age instruments, consisting of sharpened sticks for digging and cutting, arrow tips made of fire-hardened, sharpened wood, and the occasional flint knife for slashing the underbrush.

In my reading in preparation for our trip, I have learned that the creation of the Bwindi Impenetrable National Park in 1991 dealt the Batwa a severe blow. To establish the park, the Ugandan government evicted them suddenly and summarily from their ancient lands. At gunpoint and under threat of imprisonment, many were forced out of the park. They became squatters on land that is steep and treeless with brown dirt covered by sparse scrub brush and grass, available because it is of poor quality. They could no longer hunt and gather. They lacked clothing, medicine, and any knowledge of how to grow and cultivate crops. These hardships combined with dropping birth rates among the Batwa threaten the entire extinction of a people. Religious organizations and wealthy trekkers who came to see the famed mountain gorillas have been trying to help, yet I feel more must be done ... but what? What impact can we really expect to have on such pressing problems?

Map of Africa

I have been journaling for years. It started when, as Chief-of-Staff, I invited two psychiatrists from a nearby medical school to lead a workshop at our hospital to address physician burnout. The psychiatrists suggested journaling as a method for dealing with the long hours, the nights on call, and the stress of weighty decisions. This antidote to depression was as simple as pulling out a pad and pen and writing intentionally about circumstances and feelings.

My journaling increases as we prepare; it will continue in Africa as I chronicle the daily events and my emotions. My questions include:

What is the Batwa's story as a harshly displaced people?

How can I possibly connect with a people so dissimilar?

How can we be accepted?

What is their spirituality?

Why are we leaving friends and family and my comfortable medical practice in Northern California to assist the Batwa, a people we'd never previously heard of?

Why am I going? At age fifty-five?

With these questions turning in our minds, on a crystal-clear day in August 2000, Carol and I, with our now twenty-year-old son Josh, step out of the airplane and onto the tarmac of Entebbe International Airport, blinking in the sunlight. We're disoriented having spent more than twenty hours in too many airplanes and too many airports traveling from California, by way of London and Nairobi.

James, an elder from Kanungu village, where we will conduct our surveys of the Batwa, meets us at the airport. He is an exceedingly dark, rotund man, with a smile that is blindingly white. He looks jaunty in his khaki pants and colorful, open-collared, print shirt. He escorts us to his all-terrain Land Rover. As the three of us squeeze into the close quarters of the cab, James warns us, "It's an easy one-hour drive to Kampala, Uganda's capital, but the difficulty will be negotiating Kampala's traffic. It's not only the cars jammed together that bothers me, it's the incessant horns."

As we inch through the streets of Kampala, Josh remarks, "This more than lives up to James's description, pedestrians squeezing between the vehicles, horns blaring, traffic snarling ... and look at that motorcycle sneaking onto the sidewalk! Somehow this seems ordinary!"

Making our way out of Kampala, the traffic is replaced by papyrus swamps spreading out to the horizon. Dense, woody stalks form a sea of green where every color of bird takes up residence among the fronds.

Two or three hours later, we emerge from the swamp to find market stands selling fresh fish hung out to dry as well as roasted chickens skewered on sticks. They also sell goat meat and fried intestines— of what, we aren't sure, and are not about to find out. Tiny shacks selling plasticware and discarded Western clothing abound. Low mud huts with corrugated iron roofs sit next to fields where women dig. Children swarm the sides of the road to wave at us. Their clothing, if they have

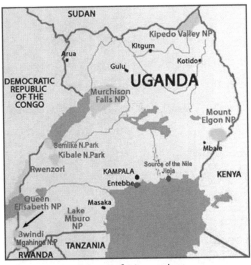

Map of Uganda

any, is torn. When we are stopped for the frequent document checks, eyes surround us on all sides, taking in our pale skin and Carol's blonde hair.

Carol anxiously notes, "Many of the kids have ringworm and other sores on their bodies. Hugging the kids may be difficult." She adds, "Your dermatology exams will certainly be easier here. Most of the kids are naked."

The only crop that seems to succeed here is bananas, specifically the East African Highland banana. Fields of them stretch for miles in all directions.

"These folks must love bananas," Josh comments.

I tell Josh, "From what I read, Ugandans consume more bananas than any other culture in the world. You'll have to get used to a diet of matoke. Matoke is produced from the green bananas that you see piled at the wayside stalls. The bananas are cooked, leeching out any nutrition. Matoke, with the addition of rice, potatoes, and cassava, a white root, will be central to our diet."

Josh is not impressed.

I add, "If the cassava is improperly prepared, then cyanide can form."

"A diet consisting of starches and poison doesn't sound appetizing," he says to me. We let the subject drop.

After many hours of bouncing along on the potholed road, we pass Mbarara, the second-largest city in Uganda. We then turn westward towards Ntungamo. From there, the road is entirely dirt and will remain so for the next six hours, all the way to Kanungu. Despite the sparse signs of civilization on the first half of our trip, that stretch now seems positively bustling. From here to the Bwindi Impenetrable Forest, our dusty, rutted road runs almost entirely through empty

Drive to the Bwindi with our fish dinner secured on the bumper

countryside, dotted only with grass-thatched mud huts. Occasionally, a village appears. As we slow down, masses of children pour out of a school yelling at us, "*Muzungu! Muzungu!*" (mu-zun-gú, originally meaning traveler or wayfarer, but today used primarily to point to white people).

It seems as if we are the only *bazungu* (plural of *muzungu*) these kids have ever seen. The children wave excitedly. Carol comments, "I feel like a homecoming queen."

We cross a narrow bridge and come upon the steep plateaus where we can look south to see the territory where Dian Fossey studied the mountain gorillas. We are now in the string of East African volcanoes, the Virunga Mountains that run along the borders of Rwanda,

The Virunga Mountains

the Democratic Republic of the Congo (DRC), and Uganda. Some of these volcanoes pierce the clouds at over fourteen thousand feet.

Buses race past us at unreasonable speeds. We're on a one-lane road, so we carefully scoot to the side and are treated to a view of the dark, muddy river one thousand feet below, a height that could inspire vertigo. As Josh peers over the edge, he comments, "I used to think guardrails were eyesores, but they would look beautiful here."

We stop only once for a meal.

"Hey, Mom, what do you think this meat is?"

Carol just laughs and gives Josh a smile as she wanders off in search of a pit latrine. She returns quickly, her characteristic smile gone. "If you think that this drive is a challenge, try the pit latrine. No relaxing in there, it's just a deep pit, covered with decaying planks with a tiny hole in the center. And, it's teeming with spiders! I'm not sure where we are going but I am ready to get there!"

On the road again, not exactly refreshed, we doze fitfully and wake to find that we have hours more to go. I try to drift off again. It must work because I'm jolted awake right outside the village.

At last, after more than fifteen hours, wearing the same clothes we've worn for three days, we arrive at our village home outside of Kanungu.

CHAPTER 3

✥ ✥ ✥

The Plight of the Batwa

"Lonely is one."

———— • Maasai Proverb • ————

*"In good times, friends know you,
and in bad times, you know them."*

———— • African Proverb • ————

We have come halfway around the world to survey the needs of the Batwa pygmies. I made sure to do my research before we got here so that Josh, Carol, and I have some context for the people we'll encounter.

The first written mention of pygmies came from the Egyptians more than four thousand years ago. They describe a people of short stature living near the "Mountains of the Moon" (the Rwenzori Mountain range separating the DRC and Uganda). The word "pygmy" is derived from the Greek word πυγμαιος, "Pygmaioi" via Latin "Pygmaei," meaning the distance from elbow to knuckles.

In 1904, the St. Louis World's Fair hired Samuel Verner to bring back African pygmies for the exhibition. One pygmy named Ota Benga was brought to the United States for display. When he returned to Africa, he found that his entire tribe had been exterminated and he asked Verner to send him back to the United States. In 1906, he became part of a new show at the Bronx Zoo. Ota Benga was exhibited in a cage in the Monkey House. The exhibit attracted up to forty thousand visitors a day and sparked vehement protest. In March 1913, he borrowed a gun and shot himself.

Today, most pygmies live in a narrow band of rain forest from Cameroon westward to the DRC, with smaller communities within the DRC and within Central African Republic to Uganda and Rwanda. The Batwa, a pygmy tribal group, are the most eastward of the pygmies, residing in the eastern DRC, southwestern Uganda, and parts of Rwanda.

As its name implies, the Bwindi Impenetrable Forest is accessible only on foot and, even then, with great difficulty. The biodiversity of plants and animals is staggering. In my passing interest in birds in the U.S., I have seen and identified around fifty species. In this small niche of Africa, there exist at least 350 species! Perhaps the region's most notable denizens are its primates. The forest is a sanctuary for Colobus monkeys, chimpanzees, and about half of the world's population of mountain gorillas.

In 1991, UNESCO designated 331 square miles of the Impenetrable Forest as a World Heritage site to protect the forest's mountain

Batwa in traditional clothing

gorillas, an endangered species. Suddenly, the Batwa were evicted from their ancient home and park rangers were given permission to shoot any who remained in the forest. The Batwa, effective immediately, became conservation refugees. They were totally disenfranchised, receiving no property, homes, food, clothing, or other compensation for their eviction. The Batwa were essentially left to die, becoming an endangered species themselves.

Forced to live in closer proximity to civilization, they contracted diseases such as tuberculosis, measles, tetanus, and typhoid. The mortality rate for Batwa children under five climbed to 38 percent, their life expectancy standing at a shocking twenty-eight years. Although the Government of Uganda identified the Batwa's plight as a national problem and promised compensation for the Batwa, that support never came. This is the situation the Batwa face, the people we are meant to help when we arrive.

Our new home is a tiny cinder-block house next to the home of Bishop John Wilson Ntegyereize, which serves as the headquarters of the Anglican Diocese of Kinkiizi. My Lord Bishop, as he is known, is a large, stern, imposing man with ebony skin. Despite the hardships of his people, he's clearly not missed many meals. Aside from his modern clothing, he reminds me of an African chief presiding over his village.

My Lord Bishop, as he is known, is a large, stern, imposing man with ebony skin. Despite the hardships of his people, he's clearly not missed many meals. Aside from his modern clothing, he reminds me of an African chief presiding over his village.

He is wearing a dress shirt with the signature white collar, appropriate for an Anglican bishop, worn under an immaculately tailored dark suit. Around his neck hangs a heavy, gold cross suspended from a chain. With a wide, toothy smile, he greets us, "*Webare kwiija*." Sensing my confusion, he continues, "That's welcome in our language." As I grasp his huge, manicured hand, I spot a large, expensive-looking gold watch.

A visit with Bishop John Wilson Ntegyereize and his wife, Jocelyn

Bishop John introduces his wife, Jocelyn, whose four daughters surround her. Jocelyn is a beautiful, somewhat heavyset woman with close-cropped hair. She has smooth, flawless skin and a welcoming smile.

Although his greeting is warm, we quickly sense that Bishop John isn't a natural charmer. While his British English delivers words of welcome, his demeanor seems to shout, "This is my house. This is my diocese. You are welcome only as long as you follow my rules." We respond as we sense we should, amiably and deferentially.

When we suggest that we locate to a Batwa village to be closer to our research and to learn some of their language, he adamantly refuses. "It simply isn't safe. You are the only *bazungu* in a several-hundred-mile radius. You might be the targets of violence and looting. Only here, under my watchful eye, can I assure your safety and you WILL return by sunset every day.

He seems to relent when I explain that on some days, when a return is impossible, we will need to sleep in a tent overnight.

With an incredulous look, the bishop responds, "*Bazungu* can live like the Batwa in a small hut?"

He seems even more confused when I attempt to explain that many *bazungu* prefer this accommodation when they vacation in the parks of the U.S.

The bishop suggests that James show us to his preference for our living quarters. The structure is a scant 250 square feet. A small bed, covered with a thin worn blanket, occupies a stark bedroom; the living room contains a threadbare couch and a wooden chair; and the tiny kitchen has a propane oven. Carol lets out a squeal when she looks in the bathroom, "A toilet. Wahoo!" I hear the woosh of water, "It even flushes!"

When we are alone, I lament to Carol, "My Lord Bishop is attempting to thwart our plans to live and learn from the Batwa."

Before we collapse into the tiny bed, Carol deftly sweeps away a large beetle with a snapping beak. Josh stretches out on the couch. Our slumber is only fitful as the quiet of the night is pierced by a cacophony of strange sounds emanating from the countryside.

We have scheduled six weeks in Africa, the last two climbing Mount Kenya. That gives us a little less than four weeks to gather our vital information before my assignment deadline. The area where we reside is mainly populated by 250,000 Bakiga (pronounced ba-cheé-guh), a neighboring tribe to the Batwa. The Batwa number around 3,500, distributed through multiple settlements surrounding the Bwindi Impenetrable Park. The needs survey we are conducting will assess rates of mortality, particularly among children aged five and under, as well as the causes of their death. Based on the survey, we will attempt to identify potential medical interventions to improve survival. While I am the person designated to formally conduct the survey and supply the medical information, Carol and Josh will provide the critical functions of gathering patient histories and attempting to negotiate the nuances of the Batwa's culture.

At daybreak, the three of us prepare for our first daylong visit to a Batwa settlement. Carol and I run through our checklist: notebooks (check), camera (check), survey forms (check), tape recorder (check). Carol adds, "Let's not forget our smiles—and open hearts and minds."

Our smiles quickly evaporate when our driver, James, arrives to report, "Your vehicle has a dead battery. Perhaps tomorrow or the next day will be better."

He waves to us jovially and begins to walk away.

"Isn't there another option?" I ask in a panic.

"No, I'm sorry," he replies. "We'll try again tomorrow."

Carol whispers, "I can't believe James is ready to call it quits."

I yell at his departing frame, "Hey James, what about another vehicle?"

He stops and turns, looking thoughtful, and says, "Yeah, I am sure that there is another vehicle we could use. The bishop has several."

Within fifteen minutes, we are on the road. James and Carol are in the front seat of the pickup. Josh and I stand in the bed of the truck, bumping along and passing women singing and carrying hoes with kids strung to their backs, walking to their fields.

"We're going to Kitariro," James announces.

"Where is Kitariro?" Carol asks.

"About a one to two hour's drive."

"Why Kitariro?" Carol persists.

"Kitariro is the closest settlement," James yells over the roar of the engine.

After an hour of being tossed around like bananas taken to market, we reach a turn-off that shouldn't be a turn-off at all. There is no signage and no milepost. Actually, there's no road. Our gray truck is now brown, covered in a thick coat of dust. We plunge into the forest, unsuccessfully attempting to avoid deep ruts. The truck bounces hard and then swerves downward around several bends.

Passing through the trees, we spot the occasional hut. At the crest of a hill, James suddenly turns off the engine. No one moves.

"Is this it?" Josh asks me.

I shrug.

I look around. To our left I see what must be an Anglican church. From a tiny outbuilding next to the church, a small man in a clerical uniform emerges. He bounds towards us. Leaping into the bed of the pickup, he smiles an enormous white grin while giving me a generous handshake. "I am Pastor Enos, I will be your interpreter."

He continues matter-of-factly, "I will be your constant companion; you and I will be friends."

The engine roars to life and we round the hilltop. Josh, Enos, and I study the valley beyond. Spread out below is an assortment of little huts, scattered in a sort of circle, with smoke curling out of roofs of straw. Off to the side, just a stone's throw from this little village, are two larger structures. One is made of mud and thatch; I take it to be a school because of the children nearby. The other is the tiny, deserted clinic.

Though it seems as if we're virtually on top of the village, the road winding down from the church makes for a slow, harrowing drive of about ten more minutes. We finally arrive in the large, open field in front of the school.

Familiar shouts of "*Muzungu! Muzungu!*" bring more children pouring out of the building. Across the abandoned soccer field, the adults of the village rush towards us.

"I guess we're the only act in town," I whisper to Josh as I jump out of the truck bed.

Within minutes, forty or fifty people, approximately half the population of the village, surround us. When Carol, with her blonde hair, slides out of the cab, the children erupt with sounds of wonder and delight.

She smiles back at them.

We are surrounded by a sea of curious onlookers with warm, wide smiles. I know immediately that these are the Batwa. They are dressed in hand-me-down t-shirts and cut-off shorts that look like scraps pulled from Salvation Army bins. Some wear woven cloth in all manner of patterns and colors, wrapped around their bodies in clever ways. Some have tied the fabric into thick, elaborate knots around their heads. Their impish smiles are full of crooked teeth set into deeply lined faces. All are barefoot, their feet nearly white from calluses and scrapes, having walked barefoot every day of their lives.

Physically, their features are somewhat similar to the Bakiga, but the Batwa are shorter in stature, all ranging from four to five feet in height. Their faces are flatter, with larger, more pronounced jaws. Their bright demeanor and arresting presence quickly eliminates the word "pygmy" from our vocabulary. The word had seemed derogatory to us and certainly doesn't suit these vigorous, big-hearted people.

I mention to Josh, "Some anthropologists believe that we are all descended from pygmies."

Josh smiles, "It appears that we are derived from good stock."

The Batwa begin patting our backs and saying "*agandi!*" (á-Gan-dí – hello). They laugh riotously when they hear a *muzungu* attempting to speak their language.

We scan our surroundings and see that we are standing in the middle of a soccer field. Steel poles and tattered nets are positioned at each end, but there's neither a ball nor a blade of grass in sight. A creek ripples at the base of the hill. Green, rolling hills rise around the field towards a sky full of gray, dramatic clouds. On the other side of the creek, the hills are covered with dense stands of majestic trees. It's the Bwindi Impenetrable Forest, the Batwa's ancient home.

The school before us is marked with a sign that reads: MISSION FOR ALL. I steal a glance at the clinic building, its shutters dangling from broken hinges. Dried mud fills gaps in the walls and long grass protrudes from crevices. With the facility in such disrepair, I wonder to Carol if anything of value will be found inside. Carol smiles, "The value to be found here is in the people."

There are no other amenities in the village, no stores or services of any kind. Their homes are small, triangular huts that look a bit like tents constructed with tree branches interwoven with grass, leaves, and straw. These structures are private residences, each with small garden plots to the side and seating areas in front. Though some have doors, none have glass. The windows are holes hollowed out between the branches.

Enos helps us exchange introductions with the elders. He tells us, "Please introduce yourselves. I'll help."

I begin, "My name is Scott."

Enos suggests, "*Nibanyetta* (Ní-ban-yetá) Scott."

The Batwa respond, "Scort?"

Enos chuckles, "That's as close as they can get."

"I am a doctor," I say, looking at Enos.

Enos says, "*Ndi oumshaho*" (N-dí omu-Sha-hó).

The Batwa repeat, "Ah *omushaho*," with wide smiles.

"And this is, Carol,"

"Karo," the Batwa repeat.

"She is my wife."

Enos translates, "*Omukazi wangye*" (omú-Ka-zí wan-Gí). I give Carol a hug.

The Batwa look uncomfortable.

Enos explains that in this culture, affection is not expressed publicly.

"We'll adjust," Carol whispers with a laugh.

Carol tells the Batwa, "I am a teacher."

Enos encourages, "*Ndi Omushomesa*" (N-dí omú-shó-mesa).

The Batwa repeat *omushomesa*. They seem excited, greeting the news with applause.

Josh steps forward, "I am Josh."

Enos whispers to Josh who repeats, "*Ndi* Josh."

"Josh" is echoed by the Batwa. His name is easier for them to pronounce.

"I am a student."

"*Ndi omweegi*" (N-dí om-Wé-gí), Enos suggests.

Smiles all around.

Josh then tells the Batwa, "I love playing the drum".

Instantly, when Josh repeats Enos's translation, "*Ninkunda kuterra engoma,*" the Batwa explode with vigorous cheering.

Josh has learned African drumming while a student at the University of Oregon. That particular skill now appears to be a great investment.

I am surprised when several Batwa quickly race off.

I continue: "We are from America." Enos prompts me with "*Naruga* (N-du-Gá) *Amerika.*"

They look at each other quizzically and among their comments I hear, "*Merica.*"

"Where is America?" Enos asks, voicing the question the villagers are asking.

How do I explain? "It's across the ocean," I say feebly.

Enos relays their puzzled response, "Ocean? What is the ocean?" They have heard of America but not in a way that they can put into any geographic context. They seem barely aware of the nearest villages, let alone the vastness of the ocean. Anything outside of a walk of a few hours is almost unimaginable.

I am rescued from further explanations when the distant sounds of drumming increase in intensity. The Batwa, who had suddenly departed, return with several drums, which they offer to Josh and Enos.

Enos and the Batwa hammer out a traditional rhythm that he says is uniquely Batwa. Josh replicates their traditional rhythm but also demonstrates a few novel beats from other regions of Africa. Women and men join in dancing and singing, exuding joy.

They attempt to teach us how to dance with moves that are performed almost entirely with the lower half of the body. I'm not Elvis, and the hip moves feel like I'm trying something from another world. When I ask what the dance is, Enos explains: "Watch closely. The dancers use their legs to pound the earth in sequence with the drumbeat. The dust rises, and you feel the earth shake; they're communicating with the depths of the earth."

The drumbeat swells as drums are passed around. Everyone, young and old, either plays, claps, or dances. They appear to be competing, trying to one-up each other with their dance steps.

Women bring out sitting mats and bowls of food. There's the mash, matoke, as well as other fruits such as mango, papaya, and passion fruit. There's also a brownish-white, tasteless, tuberous vegetable that I learn is cassava. They are glad to share everything they have.

The Batwa have welcomed us with smiles, drums, dancing, and food, but something else is in the air. There is a tension, some reservation that is palpable. When I raise my concerns with Enos, he explains, "The Batwa are wondering, 'Do you have ulterior motives? Why are you really here? What do you want from us?'" Enos continues in a somber tone, "Other aid organizations have come before. They take photos of the Batwa and then depart. They raise money with the photos and their stories, but those donations are never returned to the tribe."

Enos's face saddens, "It isn't obvious anymore who can be trusted. Perhaps we, too, just want to photograph the mountain gorillas and the Batwa and give nothing in return."

Carol's eyes widen. We both feel the shame settling over us. How can we be different than the *bazungu* who have come before us?

With Enos's help, I explain to them, "We are working with Diane Stanton to conduct a survey to learn more about you so that we may help you." The mention of Diane, who, in conjunction with the diocese in Dallas, has purchased the land on which we are standing, wins us a measure of approval.

Carol quickly adds, "We are here to follow up on her good work, to discover what has helped and to assess what more can be done."

The tension doesn't melt away, but their guard drops a bit. We allow ourselves a measure of relief. I am ready to begin my survey of their medical conditions.

"Where do we start?" I ask.

"Ngaha" (N-Gá-há, meaning "No"), they say. "You must tell us more about yourselves."

"Do you have other children?"

"Tell us about your parents."

"Tell us about your friends."

"Tell us about your goats and chickens."

"Tell us about *Merica*."

Extended introductions are important to the Batwa. Nothing can take place until we are properly acquainted. Of all the things they want to know about us, they are most interested in our family. Enos comments, "The Batwa believe that relationships make us who we are."

We tell them as much as we can, confessing that we have no goats or chickens. We drum and dance and eat and laugh. A real warmth begins to grow.

When it comes time to begin our work, we gather in front of the abandoned clinic under the shade of a huge, lone ficus tree that has been spared the ax. The tree's branches spread out, rising a hundred feet above, providing us shelter from the elements and also serving as a home to a myriad of bird species. As we move around the Batwa lands, these magnificent ficus trees will be our home bases, our conference rooms for meetings, and the spot for collecting vital personal information. Under the ficus, many relationships will be forged.

Enos has more to tell us. "Ever since the forest was taken from the Batwa, the Batwa have resided in lands belonging to the Bakiga."

He explains, "The Batwa have adopted both the Bakiga's language and their agrarian techniques. The Batwa were resettled in land purchased for them by a United Nations group, stretching in a near circle around the forest, leaving them close enough to look, but forbidden to touch anything inside."

Enos is a Mukiga, a singular member of the Bakiga tribe. For years, he has lived in harmony with the Batwa, and they seem to trust him. He and I are given two three-legged stools with crude leather seats. We sit under the ficus tree as a crowd gathers around us. With my clipboard and pencil in hand, I'm ready with my prepared survey:

"How many children have you had?"

"How many have survived?"

"The ones who died, what did they die of?"

Carol stands nearby helping me and interacting with the women who swarm around. About thirty people surround us as I collect information from them one by one.

I prompt the group, "I am confused as to how to call your people. I do not hear the term pygmy used." They grimace at this expression. "Nor do I hear Batwa used frequently. What do you want to be called?"

A nearby woman gently says, "Call us by our names. My name is Jacint."

Each inquiry is a collaborative effort, as one community member always seems eager to correct another's information that's inaccurate. As one woman is describing a child's death, another will interrupt: "No, no, it happens like this." The group then remembers collectively and they say, "Ah, yes, yes." Cross talk among the Batwa women is the ambient sound for the day's proceedings.

The Batwa are very cooperative, but it is difficult to obtain accurate information about past events. Although their language lacks a past tense, they do have a tense for actions that have recently happened or have occurred a few days previously; however, there is no way to specify the dates or times of events occurring in the more distant past.

Enos explains that life in the forest involves mainly immediate events. "When hungry, 'Let's get food.' If game becomes less plentiful, 'Let's move.' If someone is sick, 'Let's gather herbs.'"

This prevents us from establishing timelines for their medical histories. The women are able to tell me how many times they have become pregnant and how many of their children have died. It is common to hear a mother report that only one of her four pregnancies results in a living child. Infant deaths typically are due to *omuswiija* (omu-Swee-já), their word for malaria. All fevers are attributed to malaria, as they have no way to differentiate the fevers of typhoid, pneumonia, or dysentery from that of malaria. The stories are remarkably similar: an apparently healthy child suddenly contracts a fever and is soon lifeless.

The tragedies of their lives pour out: infants and children surviving but a few years, sisters or aunts dying in pregnancy. We come to understand that for the Batwa, such tragic events are accompanied by acceptance but not remorse. We are told several shocking stories of youths who ventured into the forest, probably for poaching, and were shot by the park rangers.

One woman relates, "My family is hungry, no food for two days. I send my son into the forest to collect some yams and honey. He does not return. I worry and I worry. One day, I see several folks come out of the forest carrying something. As they approach, I recognize a few of my son's friends. They are carrying my son's body, killed by the rangers." She tells the story without emotion, no tears, just the facts.

Tragedy like this is new to me. Having worked medically in Asia and in Central and South America, I thought I was well acquainted with death, but never have I encountered it on this scale. Here, the sheer number of deaths the Batwa face on a daily basis is beyond comprehension.

I am disconcerted by the preventable nature of these illnesses. Simple measures like good nutrition, mosquito netting, and access to clean water would protect the Batwa from starvation, malaria, or diarrhea. It's even more wrenching as this death is taking place adjacent to an idyllic rainforest.

We discover that the Batwa have a low fertility rate compared with the adjacent Bakiga tribe. They relate, "In the forest, we do not have another baby until our youngest child is able to walk." The average Batwa family has three children, quite different from the Bakiga, which average six or seven. The women tell me, "We have an herbal, natural method for preventing pregnancy, which is given by our elders." It seems to be very effective.

I sit in amazement listening to story after story of death. No family has been spared; their narratives are conveyed to me stoically.

Enos translates:

"My child is alive, and then he is dead."

"What about your next child?" I ask.

"Well, for a few years she is fine, but then she dies of *omuswiija*."

"When did the last one die?" I ask.

"I do not remember; it is in the past."

Our findings indicate that a large percentage of children, approximately 40 percent, have died before age five. For these people, in the midst of daily trauma, to possess such serenity is tremendously moving and hard to fathom.

Carol transcribes their stories. Occasionally, she is overcome with emotion and finds herself weeping. It's time for a break to decompress. We move off to talk.

Carol asks, "How can the Batwa recount such sad events without crying?"

"Perhaps they have cried all the tears that can be shed?"

She counters, "I think it's more likely they're in survival mode. If they give in to tears, how will they ever stop?"

The Batwa have a way of dealing with death that is completely different from ours. Enos explains, "They don't dwell on things; they grieve with wailing and a lot of communal support. Then they move on." It is apparent that, through sharing, their grief is dispelled, allowing them to heal.

As we resume our survey, kids pound on drums and dance. When the adults are finished being interviewed, they, too, join in the dance, seemingly unaffected by the sorrows they have just related.

An elderly woman named Mamia approaches and stares into my eyes. Although only just over four feet tall, she has a commanding presence. Mamia is nearly blind. Her milky corneas are the result of trachoma, a preventable chlamydia infection, the second-leading cause of blindness in sub-Saharan Africa. We are motioned to follow Mamia into her hut. Although unable to see well, she is exceedingly agile and scoots along with ease.

She lights a pipe and puffs off a few whiffs of smoke. Her crinkly face has a ready smile. Mamia calmly tells her tale: "Uganda is starting to fence off the lands for the park. We lose our ability to hunt game and collect fruits. We have no food for several days and my family is hungry. My two sons go into the forest to hunt. They are both killed by the rangers." Her voice trails off, "I am not allowed to get their bodies."

After her story, Mamia steps outside and begins singing and dancing, stepping lightly in Batwa fashion. Her arms move fluidly up and down like the wings of a bird. Enos tells us that it's difficult to translate her song, as English doesn't have such words. But it's something like, "In order to fly, you must release your burdens and I have many."

Mamia

CHAPTER 4

✧ ✧ ✧

Gorillas Flourishing, Humans Not

"You do not teach the paths of the forest to an old gorilla."
———— • African Proverb • ————

As we walk through the forest, we are awed by its biodiversity. There is a riot of green shades from the various species of trees, trees that are alive with activity. Monkeys clamber nearby and multi-colored birds dart in the canopy. Upon occasion, we hear the roar of the most famous and imposing resident of the forest—the mountain gorilla. Carol is puzzled when Enos relates to her, "The name 'gorilla' is derived from Greek, which means 'tribe of hairy women.'"

"Honey, I don't think that you will be mistaken here," I respond.

Enos's knowledge of the gorillas is impressive, "I feel a comradery with the gorillas. Next to chimps, they are our closest relatives. I see them laugh and grieve, show love and anger. Researchers that I have worked with believe that gorillas have spiritual feelings or religious sentiments. Gorillas form a tight community, and they are smart. They can make and use tools. Unfortunately, there are only 650 gorillas remaining. They are an endangered species; it is our duty to care for them."

Today, we are at the village of Kalehe. I've spent an exhausting morning collecting data and examining dozens of patients presenting with a wide range of diseases. I decide to take a break and stroll along a path adjacent to the Bwindi. My mind is focused on the difficult cases I have attempted to diagnose, and my eyes are adjusting to

Mountain gorilla

the darkness of the forest. My attention suddenly pivots to the bushes next to me that rustle violently and then explode. I am face to face with four hundred pounds of howling, chest pounding, muscle, fur, and claws. Its high-pitched scream echoes across the mountains as its wrath zeroes in on me. Enraged animals often present frightening visual and audible signals, but what strikes me now is the smell. Not only is it the stench of halitosis, but there is a deep musty smell of raw power and wildness. I have been warned that running from a gorilla is futile. Nothing infuriates the agile gorilla more than a fleeing *muzu-ngu*. The only hope, I've been advised, is to bend down, avoid eye contact, pretend to munch on some grass, and act subservient. In my terror, this seems like a non-starter. I appear to be the endangered species here. With fleeting thoughts about my love for Carol and whether I've updated my will, I prepare for the worst.

Suddenly, just as quickly as the beast appeared, he disappears, swallowed by the greenery. The relief is exhilarating. I thank God for my new lease on life. The forest seems brighter, the birds more melodious, and the air sweeter.

I had been informed to be on the lookout for a rogue gorilla in our vicinity who had been ejected from his troupe. The lack of female companionship had resulted in a particularly nasty disposition. When I return to the nearby village, an elderly Mutwa (the singular form of Batwa), who had heard about my encounter, approaches and indulgently explains, "This gorilla is very sad and lonely and only wants attention. You shouldn't be frightened. He is just having fun with you."

At least one of us was having fun!

When I ask the Batwa about the mountain gorillas, James, a respected Batwa elder explains, "We are accused of poaching gorillas and threatening their existence, but we live together peacefully. We revere and respect gorillas and chimpanzees. We call them *sacamunto* (Sac-a-Mun-tó – like us). We believe that they are our friends and relatives."

James, although his face is furrowed and his hair and close-cropped beard are greying, is youthful in his demeanor and his gait. Honed from numerous previous forays into the forest, his wiry and athletic frame appears ready for any adventure. He points to where I had been hiking, "The Bwindi is off limits to us."

Another Mutwa adds, mimicking pulling back a bowstring, "James is respected as a great hunter. His arrow can hit a bird sitting on the top of a tree."

We are invited to enter a Batwa hut. Carol and I squeeze into a structure the size and design of a small pup tent, roughly five feet in height, constructed of leaves and thatch attached to a skeleton of saplings. Carol is amazed that such a simple structure can house a family of six. It's all-purpose, used for sleeping, cooking, and eating.

Carol comments that the villagers look very similar, and she asks if they are all related. Margaret, an aging, exceeding diminutive but very spry Mutwa woman, exits the hut and calls to several of the villagers.

One-by-one, Margaret points at the arrivals:

"This is my brother."

"These are my two sisters."

"These are my cousins and nephews."

And with a wide smile, "This is my husband."

"We all live here."

Carol replies, "In America we have a saying that it takes a village to raise a child."

Enos attempts to translate, but it is lost on a people who have been practicing this for centuries.

Carol asks Margaret how she came to live with her husband.

"He is a good-looking man from another village, whom I see now and then. I know him to be a good hunter and when he says that he likes me and wants to live together, how can I say 'no'? We hunt together, build houses together, and make decisions together."

Carol asks the Batwa, "How do you care for the elderly, the infirm, or the orphans? Do you have homes for these individuals?"

Enos has heard of orphanages and rest-homes for the elderly, but he says, "We have no words for such facilities, but I will try to ask." When Enos attempts to describe an orphanage, the Batwa become animated, talking among themselves.

"Why would someone not want to care for a child?"

"We love all our children; we raise them together!"

"Who would want to send a child away?"

The consternation continues when Enos attempts to explain to the Batwa about a home for the aged. He is quickly interrupted: "The elderly are the source of our wisdom. How can they be taken from us?"

Carol remarks to me, "What a strong sense of community."

I reply, "Folks in the U.S. frequently ask why Africa is non-functional. I'm starting to think that the Batwa can teach us much about the value of close relationships and working together as a community. These lessons will be a great gift to us."

We have many Batwa villages to visit today. Each is similar to the one before. When we reach the village of Mukono, drums, as always, announce our arrival. We locate a ficus tree and haul out our medical supplies and interview forms, and then we begin the litany of introductions. The process feels excruciatingly slow, but it can't be hurried. Besides assessing the needs of the Batwa, I practice rudimentary medicine, sitting on a stool under the ficus, stethoscope around my neck. I am the lone physician.

As I unfold a small table for the medications, more than one hundred patients surround me. Most are not terribly sick, but at least five or ten are. Some would require management in an intensive care unit, were such a thing available. Disruptions are frequent. When the work feels overwhelming, the Batwa somehow sense my fatigue and interrupt the clinic with singing and dancing. I return refreshed.

Batwa dancing

My "pharmacy" consists of only a few antibiotics, several anti-parasitic drugs, pain relievers such as ibuprofen or acetaminophen, IV solution and quinine for severe malaria, and diazepam (Valium) for seizures. I must do whatever I can; referrals are barely an option. We can provide money for transportation to a government hospital, pay for expenses that they might incur, and write referral notes to hospital staff regarding the child's condition. However, the reality is that the children will never leave the village. The distant government hospitals are known for their shortage of medical supplies, general lack of compassion, and disdain for the Batwa. Telling a patient, "You should be seen in an emergency room," is out of the question. There are no other medical services available and no other options for their survival.

The following day, we visit the village of Byumba. Once again, we go through our routine of introductions, interviews, medical treatment, and survey forms. We are requested to have afternoon tea with a group of elders. I accept, but I have difficulty relaxing, as much work remains and Bishop John's curfew cannot be violated. Carol senses my disquietude and reminds me that sharing food is part of understanding these people.

We bring bread and fruit, not wanting to deprive the people of needed resources. Nevertheless, they insist on serving us some of their meager fare. We eat and thank them profusely. I ask if they have ever seen kwashiorkor? They don't know the word, but when I explain that it is a disease of starvation where a lack of proteins makes a child swell, skin peel, and hair turn red, they nod and say, "Ah, *mutuku*. It is common." Enos notes that *mutuku* is the Rukiga word for red.

After lunch, we are engulfed by patients. I ask Josh to wander through the crowd to search for red-haired kids. When Josh returns, he laments, "When I walk through the mass of patients, the mothers hold up their children, pleading for me to have a look. It's difficult to be searching for one disease when there are so many other serious problems."

Several times Josh brings me a child whom he thinks has *mutuku*. We examine the children together and if the diagnosis is starvation, we give the mothers all we have to help: vitamins, antibiotics, and deworming medication. We then arrange for additional milk to be provided—it's never enough. We give them what we can; in return we receive a glistening smile and an emphatic "*Webare Munonga*," (Wé-bar-a Mu-non-gá – thank you).

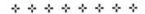

On the days we do not stay among the Batwa in our tent, we return to our house near Bishop John. We are sure to arrive before our sunset curfew and then take dinner with him and his family. We dine grandly on chicken or beef or pork. The contrast is cruel.

After returning from a clinic, as I am unpacking our vehicle, Naris, the bishop's gardener, is standing nearby accompanied by a young boy. When I notice Naris's presence, he humbly requests, "Could you please help my son?"

"Sure, what's his problem?" I respond.

"He has diarrhea."

"Anything else?"

"Only a slight cough."

"Let's take a look," I say, as I motion for Naris to bring his child into our house.

The boy is around four years old, reticent, and frightened. "He does not know *bazungu*," Naris explains.

When I sit next to him on the couch, he relaxes. He appears to be slightly undernourished, but he is generally in good health. He's taking liquids and urinating and doesn't seem dehydrated. His eyes brighten when I let him listen to his heart with my stethoscope.

Carol brings him a glass of water, which he readily gulps down. His exam is unremarkable except that I hear a little something in his lungs. It doesn't sound like pneumonia. I put him on antibiotics, adding antimalarials and an oral rehydration solution to be safe, and send him on his way, confident that he will do well.

I tell Naris, "Bring him back in the morning and let's have another look."

Naris returns at daybreak and knocks on my door.

Sleepily I ask Naris, "Where is your boy?"

"My son died last night," is his simple answer.

I am speechless and overwhelmed. After all my training and years of practice, how could I have failed to diagnose a condition that would take the life of a child within a matter of hours? I am aware that due to malnourishment and vitamin deficiencies, children have reduced immunity, and even minor ailments may prove fatal. But so quickly?

I can't meet Naris's gaze.

He humbly asks, "Please say a few words at my son's burial."

At last, summoning the courage to look into Naris's eyes, I see calm. I understand that he has accepted this outcome and will carry on. Why can't I?

That evening, as we lie together, I confess to Carol, "If Naris's son had been brought to me earlier, perhaps the result could have been different. Naris and his family live crammed in a mud hut without access to clean water or sanitation. Most of the diseases that I am treating, particularly malaria and diarrhea, are easily preventable."

Carol's next remark shocks me, "If we return to Uganda, maybe we can gather the people together and teach them how to use bed nets. Perhaps clean water systems could be helpful. Just doing some simple things might work wonders."

I doze off with her words echoing in my mind, *If we return to Uganda ... if we return.* Both of us are drawn to the Batwa. Their hope in the face of despair, their dignity despite poverty, and their sense of comradery coupled with our joy are slowly pulling us in.

CHAPTER 5

✢ ✢ ✢

Learning to Listen

"If the rhythm of the drumbeat changes,
so must the dance step."
—— · African Proverb · ——

The days are long and exhausting, draining us physically and emotionally. Of the roughly eight hundred Batwa living locally, we have managed to interview only about half of them over the course of a month. We collect data, share stories, practice a bit of medicine, and build relationships.

With Enos at my side, I am focused on gleaning the data essential to the survey. I press my questions, I offer medical treatment as needed, and I move to the next case. Like many doctors, I find myself somewhat robotic. Carol, on the other hand, is a teacher by trade, and a trained counselor. She has had conversations with the Batwa to tease out their stories.

I ask, "What is the problem here?"

"Have others in your family died?"

"How did this person die?"

Carol asks the family, "Do you have others to support you during this difficult time?"

"How does this affect you and your family?"

"Do you have sufficient food and clean water?"

These are the important questions that I've overlooked. Carol really listens, without interjecting her thoughts. She hears things that I just don't. She often simply affirms that she's listening, which produces more comfort than my medical examinations. She has discerned that several of the Batwa women lack the necessary tools for their labor and brings them pangas (machetes). It is a delightful exchange.

Carol getting to know the Batwa community

I come to realize that I can't be successful at what I do without the balance that Carol offers. I'm thankful every day to have her alongside me. Now and then, I look over at her, all twinkling eyes and wholehearted smile, laughing with a group of Batwa women or bending over to engage a child at eye level. She effortlessly shares her warmth and compassion with the exuberant and playful Batwa. The experience gives me a renewed appreciation of the love we share.

After dinner one evening, I diligently tabulate our statistics. I notice that Carol is more reserved than normal. Gazing out an open window to the darkened forest, she relates that it is difficult for her to grasp the despair of a woman named Hope. Hope's son was shot when he ventured into the forest. Or Jane, who had multiple pregnancies but remains childless. Or Florence, whose family is on the verge of starvation. Recovering her smile, she turns to me and wonders why, despite these circumstances, these folks are continually singing and seem to be so happy. "I'm learning a lot about joy from the Batwa," she concludes.

Only a few weeks into our stay, she begins alluding to other things we might do here or to other approaches we might take. "If we ever come back, we could do some real good. Your medical skills would be useful, and I could help set up schools."

I respond that I am reasonably satisfied with my U.S. medical practice and that we have gotten to a stage in life during which we can relax. "We should leave this work for the younger set," I insist.

Carol laughs, "You are still putting in huge work hours in California, it doesn't seem that relaxing to me."

Carol is right about my work, but I persist, "The needs are great all around the world and even in our hometown. Why here?" She doesn't respond.

A few days later, over a dinner of peanut butter and crackers, she says, "I have been thinking about your question, 'Why here?' The only answer that makes sense to me is that my heart is telling me I have come home."

She moves toward me and holds me tightly, saying "When we return to the United States, I want us to seriously consider the possibility of selling our belongings and relocating here."

My wife has been reluctant to visit Africa for decades out of fear of disease, violence, and the unknown. But now, she is willing to engage on a deeper level than I am. She's talking about a new life here in Africa!

It's the proverbial, heart-stopping moment. I'm completely speechless.

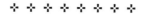

The contrast between medical practice in the U.S. versus Uganda could not be starker. In the U.S., my practice is filled with patients suffering from chronic diseases that are frequently the result of prosperity: too much food, too little exercise, too much stress. These conditions require a lifetime of medications. Patients religiously take their blood pressure medications, cholesterol-lowering agents, or diabetes drugs, but they continue living excessively.

In Uganda, I see the ugliest infectious diseases that can have dreadful consequences, but if caught early enough, they are easily treatable. A child will arrive in a comatose state from cerebral malaria. With treatment, the child will typically wake the next day, eat the day after, and in three to four days, walk home with no residual effects. The experience is exhilarating. Furthermore, if the results are not what we expect or hope, and even if the patient doesn't survive, the response is always "Thank you." The gratitude, which often feels unearned, is humbling and overwhelming. This is the practice of medicine in its rawest and, perhaps, truest form.

Here in Africa, there's no risk of an administrator coming to me saying, "You could have been more diligent in your use of resources," or, "You have to be more efficient with your practice, see more patients, spend less time just talking with them."

Every human body is different, and every human has a unique way of communicating their story. I have to listen and be present with people because the correct diagnosis hides in their imprecise language. This I learned in medical school, but in the U.S., it is easily forgotten. Only about 15 percent of the time does a physical exam yield a correct diagnosis; an additional 5 percent of diagnoses derive from subsequent lab work. The other 80 percent? That's in what the patients tell me. They can't put the name to their ailment. They talk only in their own language. To discern their problem, I have to listen for the subtleties, the words used or not used, to describe what they are experiencing. Only then can I identify the problem.

It all starts with patients talking and me listening. Studies have indicated that U.S. physicians, after asking patients to express their concerns and to tell their story, listen for an average of eighteen to twenty-three seconds before they interrupt in some fashion. Most physicians do not ascribe to the stoic Zeno's dictum: "We have two ears and one mouth, so we should listen more than we speak."

Privacy is not valued in Uganda; there are no enclosed spaces for discrete conversations. I sit on a stool under a ficus tree, Enos by my side, Carol nearby, and patients and their relatives closely packed around us. Everybody is working together for one purpose—healing—and everyone is interested. A patient will begin to tell me their symptoms and concerns, only to be interrupted by a nearby relative or friend, "No, it didn't happen that way." They openly discuss the problem at hand, no holds barred. They freely discuss relationships, and even sexual issues! No secrets, no confidentiality, true camaraderie. Slowly but surely, amid raucous laughter, pointed questions, and a physical exam behind a hanging sheet, a diagnosis emerges.

The time of day loses importance. It's irrelevant. There are no appointments. I'm rediscovering what initially drew me to medicine. Everything I learned in school is put into practice: the physical exam, the patient history, the nonverbal clues, the potential importance of every sign and symptom. Here, I think, I can be the doctor I always wanted to be.

I've never worked harder or longer than I have in these few short weeks, but it has refreshed me. I'm coming alive. Moreover, I have found unforeseen gifts. Time spent among the Batwa, people who find reason each day to celebrate being alive, is infectious. Nothing is more important to us, or more pressing, than the immediacy of our lives together. Being here is a great gift for Carol and for me.

But coming to live in Africa? I lie awake, turning the idea over in my head. I know that, professionally, I have been incredibly fulfilled in our short time in Uganda. However, I wonder if I'm ready to close up shop, to say goodbye to life in the states. The work in the U.S. has been good to me. I've loved my patients and the community where I work. I live in one of the most beautiful areas of California where I can hike and fish and then walk into town for a latte. Returning to Africa for short visits would be easy, and yet, the idea of returning on a permanent basis keeps coming up. Should I listen?

We have been working for almost a month, and soon, we will be departing for Mount Kenya. After dinner, Carol, Josh, and I are sitting outside, and the conversation turns to the possibility of returning to work and live in Uganda.

"From a practical perspective, the needs are so great and our efforts are so small, can we really make a difference?" I begin. "Patient care requires a coordinated effort, especially with the Ugandan government for referrals and supplies. Haven't we done the job we came to do? Don't you think that it's time to return home?"

"I don't think that we can count on the government. They are doing very little for the Batwa and may never assist," Carol counters. She pauses, then adds, "I've seen each day what we are accomplishing. We have made a difference. If we don't help the Batwa with their problems, they may soon cease to exist. How can we not assist?"

Josh agrees, "The simplest of things help a lot. Mosquito nets. Sanitation and water. Improved diet. These people are dying from malaria, malnutrition, and other preventable problems. You could do something about that. You could be their educators and advocates."

Carol piles on, "I'm a teacher. If we were to live here rather than supporting the cause from the U.S., we could teach them about sanitation, nutrition, and show them a path to health. You could address the medical issues and I could teach. Together we could do something significant."

I reflect on life here. Although our living conditions have been exceedingly basic, they are freeing. Having lived in a cramped tent, unable to avoid pressing issues, Carol and I now face all difficulties as a team. We talk long into the night, decompressing from the day's challenges. We appreciate each other's insights and thoughts—and we're reconnecting.

Carol comments, "The simple lifestyle and taking each day's problems as they come is quite a pleasant change from our life in California."

I lean back, looking at the stars twinkling above. I recall my interactions with the Batwa and how much I am learning, not only about their lives and their sense of community, but about my own life and my relationship with my family. The work has been fulfilling for me as a doc and Carol as a teacher, and for both of us as a couple. While there are privations around the globe, the Batwa's need is compelling. It is apparent that I have the training and skill set to help address the Batwa's challenges, yet I also realize that need does not constitute a call. As a follower of Jesus, I try to open my heart to listen to God's intentions for my life. When I look deeply, it is obvious that my heart has been opened in ways that could only be Divinely inspired.

I look over at my son and my wife, taking a deep breath before I say, "I think we're hearing a call."

✢ ✢ ✢ ✢ ✢ ✢ ✢ ✢

We return to the U.S. and take stock of our lives.

When I approach my colleagues asking their opinions regarding moving to Uganda, I receive only a few supportive replies. Most of their curt comments range from the negative to the very negative.

"What, Africa, at your age?"

"You're giving up too much!"

"What about your income?"

"It would be impossibly stressful on you and Carol."

"Practice medicine in Uganda? You're kidding, right?"

"All alone in Africa, no other docs?"

"That's crazy talk."

I really shouldn't be surprised. As chief-of-staff at the hospital, I had recently given the medical staff a satisfaction survey. Aware of discontent among a number of physicians, I thought that I needed to get a sense of their attitudes toward work. The results indicated that some 24 percent of the doctors were exceedingly happy with their profession and loved their medical practice. Another 58 percent were content but considered the medical profession a job and not a calling. The other 18 percent were severely burned out; they found no delight in their work and had entirely lost the joy of the doctor-patient relationship.

I understood this loss. Honestly, the sheer volume of administrative details was overwhelming me. The practice, chief-of-staff duties at the hospital, work at the indigent clinic, and weekend church activities kept me extremely busy for well over sixty hours per week. Were the presumed hardships of Africa more exhausting than this?

While my medical colleagues are not so supportive of our ideas about moving to Africa, it is a different case with our friends, particularly our church friends. They are willing to relax over a cup of coffee and listen.

"How many times does a person get a chance to do such good in the world?"

"What a terrific opportunity at this stage in your life to do something exciting that will have such impact."

"Jesus said, 'What you do for the least of your brothers and sisters you do for Me.' These Batwa are those brothers and sisters who need you."

"It sounds to me like your mind may not be made up, but your heart is. I'd follow your heart."

After such discussions with friends and relatives, and several months of reflection and prayer, Carol and I conclude that it is right for us to move to Uganda. The logistics are challenging. We sell the hospital that I had acquired with two other medical colleagues. We also unload our 2,400-square-foot residence and our 3,000-square-foot ski cabin, and squeeze into our newly constructed five-hundred-square-foot, one-room, minimalist cottage, storing most of our possessions.

One evening, as we sit on our cottage porch overlooking the creek, Carol tells me that she misses some of our warehoused possessions. I jokingly ask her, "Okay, let's try to recall the stored articles; whatever we can't recall, let's jettison." I am startled when Carol agrees with the plan. Over several days we list what we can remember. When we compare our list with the inventory at the storage facility, we are surprised how many of our possession we have simply forgotten about. We decide to sell these in yard sales or donate them.

Leaving our "stuff" turns out to be easy, leaving family is far more difficult. Our two sons are engaged in studies in other parts of the United States. Our summers together have been filled with hiking, fishing, and swimming. Our holidays together are happy events, eagerly anticipated. We will greatly miss our friends. Carol's elderly mother is living alone, and we won't be able to care for her from distant Africa.

We initially commit to spend a couple of years in Uganda living with the Batwa; although, it's clear that we could be there considerably longer. As we leave for this extended time, we can't help but worry that leaving our home for a remote part of the globe will be detrimental to our friendships. Little do we know that the community of Nevada City and Grass Valley will become fully engaged in our work in Uganda. Many of the projects in Uganda will be initiated through their generosity and support. The ties to family, friends, and our community will ultimately be strengthened when so many will come to visit us in Uganda and join us in supporting the Batwa.

CHAPTER 6

✦ ✦ ✦

Finding our Voice

*"Kindness is a language which the blind can see
and the deaf can hear."*

———— • African Proverb • ————

After a year's absence, Carol and I return to the Bwindi. The Batwa joyously greet us with dancing and singing, welcoming us as old friends, *"Mugarukire! Mugarukire!"* (Mu-gar-u-Chí-ri – You have returned! You have returned!). We sit together and, as we talk, we come to understand that the best way we can engage the Batwa is simply spending as much time as possible at each settlement. Although we have access to the house next to the bishop, many nights per week we pitch our tent at a Batwa settlement and are diligent about learning their stories, language, and traditions.

We are excited about working with the Batwa and are given assurances that there are others who will come alongside us. The Ugandan government has expressed an interest and seems remorseful about driving the Batwa from the forest. We have also talked with several non-governmental organizations (NGOs) in southwest Uganda whose mission is to assist the Batwa. We had looked forward to a vibrant relationship with these groups; it is apparent to us that we can't do this work alone. Unfortunately, these anticipations set us up for huge disappointments.

As it turns out, the NGO and Uganda government officials are loath to assist the Batwa. When we visit them in their headquarters in

Carol and Scott's campsite

Kampala, they frequently hint at, or else directly ask, "What's in it for us?" Their polite name for this extortion is "facilitations."

In one such visit, we enter an imposing edifice to meet with a government official who is in charge of education. We anticipate exploring how we might partner in educating the Batwa. The waiting room is packed, standing room only. Carol mentions that, thankfully, she has a few snacks in her purse, as it appears we will be here for a while. We are surprised when a well-dressed, portly secretary approaches us and announces, "The assistant minister of education will be delighted to see you." As we make our way through the throng, Carol enquires about the other patrons who have been waiting longer. "Oh, they understand that our government is not efficient."

We are led into a spacious office and warmly greeted by a stocky man wearing an expensive, well-tailored suit and flashy shoes. After greetings and a profuse handshake, he asks, "How can I help?" We relate our well-rehearsed discourse about the plight of the Batwa, adding that one of the most important routes to their survival and sustainability is through education. "Glad that you mentioned education," he interrupts, furrowing his brow. "I have two sons who are very smart. They are getting a fine education at a private university; however, their school fees are exorbitant." Hanging his head dejectedly, he offers, "What's a poor man like me to do?"

I tell the official that I will pray for him and for his sons. As we exit the office empty handed, Carol remarks that he'd rather have our cash than our prayers.

In our tent at night, Carol frets, "I don't know what I was thinking when we decided to return. I feel that we are abandoned."

I reply, "Perhaps this is God's way of letting us feel, in small measure, what the Batwa are experiencing."

With spirits low, we indulge in a moment of self-pity, sharing some tears. We've sold our possessions and relocated to assist a forgotten people, but we seem to be alone in the venture. We hit an emotional wall.

When we meet with several of the Batwa elders, they are not at all surprised that we are having difficulty in getting people to collaborate on projects meant to benefit them. They sympathize with our feelings of being overwhelmed and seem to understand what we need. "*Otafayo, uza kuguma aha*," (Otaa-Faa-yo, U-za ku-Gu-ma Ah-ha – Don't worry, just stay with us). It seems a good plan to us, especially since our other efforts have been so unrewarding. They continue advising us, "*Kwonka, nitubassa kushomesa orukiga*," (But, you have to learn to speak Rukiga – pronounced ru-Chee-ga).

In researching their language, we discover that the Batwa lost their indigenous tongue generations ago. It is typical for pygmies throughout Africa to embrace the language of the adjacent and dominant tribal group with whom they trade. As a result, the Batwa have adopted Rukiga, the language of the dominant Bakiga tribe.

Enos, our trusty translator, has been terrific, but Carol and I laugh about difficulties that we have had with translation. A Mutwa might speak for several minutes regarding her opinion on a particular subject. When she finishes, we ask Enos, "What did she say?"

Enos replies: "She says, 'No.'"

We realize that language acquisition is an essential window into the Batwa's world, yet we know it will be a challenge for us to learn. Rukiga has eleven different noun groups, and the sentence structure revolves around the noun. The verbs, adjectives, and adverbs also change with respect to the eleven noun groups. Adjectives are particularly difficult, as they change twenty-two different ways, depending on whether the noun is singular or plural. For instance, a big white person is "*muzungu muhango*" (M-zun-gú mu'-Hang-go), but a big dog is "*embwa mpango*" (M-bwá m-Pang-go). I can't fathom how an uncomplicated people developed such a complicated language!

To help with the language, we obtain a phrase book: *English to Runyankore: Easy Reading Handbook.* Runyankore (run-yun-Ko-lē) and Rukiga are similar Bantu languages. The book is only about twenty-five pages long and appears to have been printed on a home mimeograph machine. It contains only the simplest of phrases. Carol and I chuckle at a few handy expressions:

"*Nkaita enjoka nyenka.*" – I kill a snake alone.

"*Embwa yamutuma.*" – He has been eaten by a dog.

On page three, we encounter a section bearing the bold title "**Death**." Here are a host of words and phrases that we have heard the Batwa use frequently.

"*Aitsirwe ki?*" – What is the cause of death?

"*Atwiire arwaire obwire buriingwa?*" – Has he/she been sick for long?

"*Kanekizibu okufeerwa!*" – What a pity!

"*Omuntu ondiijo afire.*" – Another person has died.

Indeed, a third of the book's "Useful Phrases" section is comprised of words related to death, pain, or suffering. These are ever-present aspects of the Batwa's life.

This may seem dark, but we find that the Batwa typically see it from another side. We had asked an elderly man, who seemed to have a persistent smile etched on his face, "Why are you so happy?" He responded that his happiness came from surviving the night, and finding himself alive in the morning, "If I awake and am alive, I have to rejoice and sing."

Impoverishment and death are pervasive, yet we see little depression among the Batwa. We find that it is the rare patient who might benefit from antidepressant medications. I contact a psychiatrist friend in the U.S. regarding my findings. After hearing more about the Batwa's language, he informs me, "Having no past or future tense will influence the way a person thinks and what they think about. If they have no language structure that allows them to dwell on difficulties of the past and no tense to express anxieties about the future, depressive thoughts will be rare." He adds with a chuckle, "I charge $250 per hour to encourage my patients to practice mindfulness by living in the moment. These people do it naturally."

As we improve our language skills, Carol and I function more independently. I relate to my patients better and Carol begins her work regarding appropriate educational opportunities for the Batwa. Deciding to communicate more intently with the Batwa about health, Carol and I team up in an attempt to address malaria, an ever-present enemy. We gather a group of women to discuss malaria prevention, especially the use of bed nets. After introductions, I explain to the women the value of sleeping under a bed net. When I mention the words "bed net," they laugh rather hysterically.

Carol pulls me aside and says, "How can they not appreciate the virtue of a bed net to keep their children free from malaria?"

Frustrated, I ask if there are any questions.

A woman shyly raises her hand. With a large smile, she inquires, "How can sleeping under a 'speckled hen' prevent malaria?"

It appears our language skills need some fine-tuning. We realize that I have confused the very similar local words for speckled hen (*ekitembe* – E-Chi-tem-bé) and net (*ekitimba* – E-Chi-tim-bá).

We join in their full-throated laughter.

CHAPTER 7

✢ ✢ ✢

Discovering the Source

"In the beginning is Nagasan,
Today is Nagasan,
Tomorrow is Nagasan.

Who can make an image of Nagasan?
He has no body.

He is the word which comes out of your mouth.

That word!

It is no more, it is past, and still, it lives!

So is Nagasan."

—— · Congo Baka Prayer · ——

Acquiring basic language skills helps Carol and me learn about the Batwa's history, legends, and traditions. We believe that the more we know about Batwa culture, the better we will be able to understand and relate to them, and they to us. The Batwa are a spiritual people; their beliefs play a strong role in their daily lives. They are famous for storytelling but are very circumspect in discussing their lore. They advise us, "Only in the forest can we tell our ancient legends."

Now, removed from the forest, their legends might die. We hear of an elderly Mutwa named Jacobo who dwells at a remote settlement. Jacobo is the keeper of the Batwa's spiritual traditions and legends. We have tried on several occasions to locate him and wonder if he, too, might be a legend. However, on one trek to an area that we rarely visit, we learn that Jacobo resides nearby. We hike up a narrow, steep trail, and there, perched on a ridge above the Bwindi Forest, is a small Batwa settlement.

In the center of the village, living in a tiny hut constructed of sticks and banana leaves, lives Jacobo. His shriveled body is contorted with arthritis. He is unable to stand and moves with a painful, beetle-like crawl, dragging his shrunken legs behind him. His withered skin is covered with fly-infested sores, and he is practically blind.

We are warmly greeted with "*Agandi*," (Hello), "*Orarage*," (O-Ra-ré-gi – How was the night?), "*Oriota*," (How are you?).

We introduce ourselves, "*Nibanyetta* Scott, *na* Carol."

They repeat, "Scort *na* Karo."

He acknowledges us and, with a toothy grin, welcomes us to his village. "*Shitama aha*," (Sit here), indicating a spot next to him. Despite his obvious infirmities, Jacobo exudes an inner power and warmth. Surrounding him are some forty Batwa who bear a surprising resemblance to him. Indeed, he presents his progeny: children, grand-children, and great-grandchildren. All the people of the village are derived from his seed, and he is held in great regard.

Carol respectfully requests, "Please, can you tell us some Batwa stories and legends?"

Jacobo replies, "Only if you bring me a Coke and a blanket. Then I tell the stories. I hear about Coca-Cola and wish to have a taste. The nights are chilly here; I need a blanket to ward off the cold."

As our gear is not stocked with either item, Carol says, "We will return in a week or two."

With a smile, he says, "I wait a long time. A little longer is no problem."

Days later, we travel to a trading center and Carol picks out a very colorful, warm blanket and a bottle of Coke. Carol likes the blanket but has reservations about the soda. "The Batwa have beautiful teeth. Soft drinks won't do anything good for them."

We retrace our steps to Jacobo's village. They are expecting us. As we approach, we are warmly welcomed by singing and dancing children who grasp our hands and lead us to Jacobo's hut.

We fan out on the ground around the hut's entrance. Carol drapes the blanket over Jacobo's shoulders, and he strokes the material approvingly. As I hand him a Coke, his whole being seems to expand and he warmly gathers us in closer to him.

Carol and Scott with Jacobo and his community

He tightly wraps himself in the blanket and, looking quizzically at the Coke, enquires, "How do you open this thing?"

I show Jacobo how to pop off the cap with a bottle opener. Carol attempts to caution him, but too late, as the fizzy liquid explodes out. "This drink has energy!" he exclaims. Recovering from his fright, he takes a swig, and a broad smile spans his face. He seems to unfold from his contracted state, and, to our surprise, breaks into song. A melodious voice seems to spring from the earth itself as Jacobo sings an ancient creation legend:

"*Nagasan* (Ná-Gá-san – the God of the Batwa) forms the soil of the earth and the rain from the sky. Then the trees and vines of the forest. Then the birds, monkeys, and gorillas. Finally, *Nagasan* creates humans, designing them in a variety of colors, sizes, and shapes. *Nagasan* reflects on his creation, feels good about what is made, and then rests."

Jacobo pauses while taking another sip of Coke, then continues. "After a period of time, *Nagasan* calls all the peoples of the earth into his presence to give them gifts. Initially, the light-skinned people come, and he says to them, 'You are the first, you get the best: the fertile land with abundant game. Grow and prosper.' Next come the dominant tribal groups. 'There is much that remains, I give you the bounty of the earth, the land, and plentiful animals for hunting. Go and flourish.' The peoples of the earth are happy, healthy, and content."

The legend seems to have ended, as Jacobo drains the Coke and emits a hearty belch.

After a lengthy pause, he resumes on a more somber note. "The Batwa arrive for their gifts. *Nagasan* is surprised to see the Batwa and remarks, 'I am very sorry, but I forgot about you. All the gifts are gone, there is nothing left for you.'"

Jacobo again trails off, with the phrase, "I forgot about you" lingering in the air.

Jacobo begins singing again, more forcefully, lyric by lyric: "*Nagasan* ponders for some time, but then recalls a remote uninhabited forest. 'Ah, there is the Bwindi Forest, it is all that remains for me to give. But life is demanding in the forest; no crops can be grown. The animals are plentiful, but difficult to hunt. There are wild beasts and snakes that can bite. The nights are cold and wet. However, in order to survive, I will give you extra wits and cunning. If you are united, and work together, you will prosper. I will help you. I will give you this forest.'"

Jacobo's voice subsides. In the silence that follows, sadness washes over us.

We ponder the fact that one of the Batwa's central legends of creation reveals that Nagasan has forgotten them. And now, the only gift that Nagasan gave them, the Bwindi Forest, has been taken away! The Batwa have been neglected by Nagasan and the world.

Carol and I hold each other, sharing the Batwa's sadness. She whispers, "Blessed are the poor in spirit, for they will inherit the kingdom of heaven."

Before we leave, Jacobo looks intently at me and says, "We Batwa experience *Nagasan* when we are in the deep parts of the forest. We experience *Nagasan* at night when we look to the stars. We experience *Nagasan* in the excitement of the hunt. How do people from your country experience *Nagasan*? Do your people find *Nagasan* in all that surrounds them?"

"Unfortunately, many in America don't seek to learn from nature and experience its blessings, but rather endeavor to exploit and control it. They're afraid of places like the forest," I reply.

Jacobo and the Batwa shake their heads. "It must be so difficult in your country. The forest is very dark and cold. If you respect the forest and open your heart to it and to all its creatures, you have no fear."

"Indeed, but many are not willing to open their hearts because they are afraid that their hearts might be broken."

Jacobo grins knowingly, "We have much to teach you! Please return soon."

A few days later, we are informed that Jacobo has died.

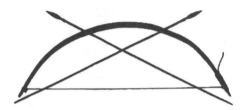

PÅRT̄ II (2001 – 2003)
Mobile Medicine

"I am not African because I was born in Africa.
I am African because Africa was born in me."

—— • Kwame Nkrumah • ——

CHAPTER 8

✦ ✦ ✦

Medical Practice
Under the Ficus Tree

*"When the master of the house lacks wisdom,
the doctor's work is useless."*

———— • Ugandan Proverb • ————

We are not sure who, if anyone, will join us in the work of caring for the Batwa. However, we do know that we have been called to minister to these people and that they are ravaged with sickness and death. Although I have served many years of medical practice and hold a master's in public health and tropical medicine, I feel unsure I am up to the challenges. Nevertheless, we do have something of a plan.

Initially, our focus will address the immediate health needs of the community while looking for opportunities to engage in preventive health. To reach the scattered Batwa villages, we purchase an aging Land Rover from an elderly British doctor in Kampala who has spent forty years in Uganda. When I ask him how he and his family survived the difficult times, particularly the years under the brutal dictator Idi Amin, he responds, "During the good times I didn't want to leave, and during the bad times, I wasn't allowed to."

As we begin to settle into our work in the Bwindi region, we are happy to become reacquainted with friends there who have been awaiting our arrival. Although we live in an isolated area, we find comfort and solace in regular communications with family, friends, and colleagues. They give us emotional support and some even participate in our work from afar, making suggestions regarding diagnoses or medical treatments. Many are deterred by the long journey to sub-Saharan Africa, but they do pass on information to students who might have an adventurous spirit. If friends and colleagues ask how they might contribute, I tell them, "If you are able to donate $1,500, then purchase a plane ticket and join us, if you have more than that, then please bring the residual with you. A visit to Uganda is a chance not only to impact a country but also to change a life— your own." Several take my suggestion seriously, to the benefit of all.

Ben Elkon is one of our first young volunteers. He is a pre-med student, who has come to study medical practice in sub-Saharan Africa. Ben and I have much to learn about one another and about medicine. Ben has closely cropped hair, the strength of an athlete, and a sharp wit. He helps us load the battered Land Rover with a tent, sleeping bag, and medical gear. Our plan is to engage in several mobile medical clinics, while camping adjacent to Batwa villages.

At the village of Mukono, we gather under a huge ficus tree on the side of a mountain slope. Many of the trees in this area have been harvested, but this giant tree, standing 150 feet tall, remains a lonely sentinel. Enos explains that this tree has been revered and used as a meeting place for generations. Ficus trees are the keystone species in many rain forest ecosystems because they sustain populations of many seed-dispersing birds that feed on their fruits. They date back over eighty million years.

As I sit under the shade, my back against the ficus, surrounded by patients, I reflect on all that the ficus has given to humanity over many millennia. From a ficus tree, Adam and Eve took leaves to cover their nakedness, and beneath a ficus tree, the Buddha became enlightened. The ficus is one of the two significant trees of Islam. The ficus tree was sacred in ancient Greece and Cyprus, where it was a symbol of fertility. When cut, the sap is a milky, white substance, likened to mother's milk in ancient Roman lore. It is under the ficus that we now practice the healing art of medicine. This ficus tree provides not only protection from the African sun but also affords supple aerial roots from which to suspend the IV bags. This tree becomes our clinic and a place for restoration, healing, and compassion.

In the area surrounding the tree, we divide the crowd into a variety of treatment zones. One area concentrates on pregnant mothers, another area focuses on children's issues, another site treats gastrointestinal parasites, and those with tropical ulcers gather at another location. Ben and I treat numerous cases of dysentery, malaria, and tuberculosis, and then a few cases of elephantiasis and other esoteric tropical illnesses. Carol calmly sits on a mat, surrounded by children, while she removes infected tissue from tropical ulcers.

Makeshift intensive care unit with IVs hanging from branches

At the base of the ficus, we establish our "intensive care unit." The severely ill patients lie on simple mats shaded and protected by this giant tree. IV tubes snake down from bags of quinine solution into the veins of several semi-comatose children. Malaria is the scourge of sub-Saharan Africa. About six hundred thousand kids, most under the age of five, die from malaria every year. Cerebral malaria is universally fatal if untreated. However, when we administer quinine, an age-old medicine, these fragile children will be allowed to live, to laugh, and to love.

At dinner, Ben is very quiet. Later, as we sit discussing the events of the day, he reads to us from his journal:

Just before daybreak, I am jolted awake from a deep sleep by a symphony of forest creatures, punctuated by the howls of colobus monkeys. I feel intimidated because my skills are so raw, but I begin to feel better when I am accompanied by two other students who are equally apprehensive.

Walking through the jungle, we carry medical supplies into a large, cleared section under a huge ficus tree, where a crowd of more than fifty is awaiting us, with more coming from every direction. The short, broad features of the Batwa clearly distinguish them from the crowd, which is mostly composed of the Bantu majority. The swollen bellies of emaciated children, the ragged clothing, the flies, the smells ... Africa washes over me in a heartbeat, overwhelming all of my senses at once. Most of those gathered around us have walked for hours to see the doctor, for a rare chance at medical attention.

The first patient we examine is a nine-year-old girl, barely conscious, lying limply in her mother's arms. We lay the girl on a straw mat under the ficus tree, and start an intravenous quinine drip, tying the IV bag above her using available vines. Next, Scott asks me to inject a man's foot with painkillers. Stepping over to a middle-aged man, I am confronted with the image of a large, bloody tumor on the outer sole of his foot. A short time after the injection, Scott and I remove the shallow growth and disinfect the wound. When finished, we hand the man several small packets of pills and dressing materials.

I take a short shift assisting Carol at the wound care area. Young patients lie on several straw mats, while others wait in a long line. They are susceptible to tropical ulcers, an infection believed to be caused by flesh-eating bacteria. The open wounds they create can grow upwards of six centimeters in diameter and eventually infect the bone.

Remarkably, these massive wounds are painless. As a result of their pain-free nature, and the inability of impoverished locals to afford even the cheapest antibiotics, the infections typically go untreated, wrapped in old rags, and ignored until infected bones weaken and break. In addition to the administration of oral antibiotics, we disinfect the open wounds and dress them. Scott taps me on the shoulder. Normally an extremely warm and jovial personality, he looks extremely serious. He wants to show me something.

A young woman, stomach bulging in pregnancy, lies semi-conscious under the ficus tree with the other critical patients. Scott tells me that she has malaria, and that the mortality rate for severe malaria during pregnancy increases to above 30 percent. Together, we start a quinine drip and try to make her comfortable. In all likelihood, she has children already waiting for her at home. There is not much time to consider her situation. Next patient....

Ben closes his journal. We sit quietly digesting his reflections. Ben breaks the silence: "This medicine is challenging but working together made it manageable. Sharing is the best part."

The following day, another medical volunteer from the U.S. joins us. He has brought bottles of soapy water and loops for blowing bubbles. Although it is a hot, sunny African day, we are rather cool sitting under the shade of the ficus tree. Surrounding us are IVs hanging from the drooping vines, dozens of patients lying on mats, and a multitude of curious children. Intense squeals of laughter resound as the globes of soap bubbles waft upward. Even the sickest patients manage to wake to watch the brilliant orbs. This is a veritable touch of magic.

An overwhelmed medical student approaches Carol in search of comfort. They sit in silence, watching the bubbles float away. Carol softly tells her, "Perhaps many of the lives of these people seem as short-lived as the soap bubbles. While on earth, though, each has his or her own radiance and joy."

CHAPTER 9

✧ ✧ ✧

Essential Medicines

"Disease and disasters come and go like rain,
but health is like the sun that illuminates the entire village."

———— • African Proverb • ————

It is common knowledge that big pharmaceutical companies push large numbers and types of cleverly named and very expensive drugs into the markets of developed countries. The marketing has been quite successful; the CDC estimates that 50 percent of adults take one or more prescription drugs daily.

By contrast, while I was studying for a master's in tropical medicine, I learned that, excepting tuberculosis and human immunodeficiency virus (HIV), 80 percent of the acute diseases prevalent in sub-Saharan Africa can be cured with a choice from a formulary of only five drugs:

- An antibiotic, like erythromycin, for bacterial infections; pneumonia, cholera, gonorrhea, trachoma.

- Praziquantel to treat schistosomiasis.

- Quinine for malaria.

- Mebendazole for nematodes (roundworms), which can sap vital nutrients, causing severe anemia. Nematodes infect two billion people worldwide, with a high prevalence in Africa.

- Metronidazole, which is used for amoebic dysentery, and is therapeutic for some bacterial infections.

Only five drugs, all widely available, can cure the bulk of infectious and parasitic diseases in sub-Saharan Africa! The Médecins Sans Frontières (MSF) *Essential Drugs* guide recommends that treatment be administered in a simple fashion: "The shortest and least divided treatments are most often recommended, single-dose or a short treatment over a few days are ideal when indicated."

Armed with an ample supply of these drugs, and the right approach, we find that we can have a significant impact on the health of a remote community when we go with a team for just one day-long clinic. On one of these visits, we are joined by our son Josh who has flown over to see us on a break from his graduate studies. Josh brings a refreshingly positive attitude and wholehearted engagement. Besides Josh, several visiting medical students on a medical outreach also accompany us today. We initially walk to the Batwa settlement of Kalehe, planning to assess the health needs there before continuing to the site of our medical clinic scheduled for today. The clinic has been publicized not only among the Batwa but also in the neighboring communities of Bakiga.

The trail to the settlement is challenging, across a forty-five-degree slope, no more than six inches wide, and very slippery. The vegetation has been hacked away with a machete, leaving six- to twelve-inch icepick-like stems protruding from the ground, waiting to impale anyone unfortunate enough to slip and fall.

When we arrive, six Batwa children are in extremis, curled on woven reed mats in a central clearing, surrounded by family members. We examine them and find that they are lethargic and febrile. Many have enlarged spleens. They have all the hallmarks of malaria; however, a few children have bloody diarrhea, abdominal pain, and constantly high fever. Villagers carry several other Batwa children to us, incapacitated with similar diarrheal symptoms. Our assessment indicates that although many are afflicted with malaria, others have the hallmarks of amebic dysentery. We learn that many of their pit latrines have collapsed from recent rains, resulting in raw sewage flowing into their water supply. They have no tools for digging new pits. Carol volunteers to walk with a few Batwa to a nearby town to purchase picks and shovels.

The kids are loaded on parents' backs, and we proceed along the trail to the site of our planned mobile clinic. A crowd of approximately one hundred patients awaits us, clustered under the shade of a giant ficus tree. More arrive, some carried on stretchers. The Batwa children from Kalahe are placed on mats at the base of the ficus tree, IVs are started, fluids are administered, quinine is given for malaria, and metronidazole is dispensed for amoebic dysentery, together with mebendazole for intestinal worms.

Villagers carrying a patient to Dr. Scott for medical attention

One medical student, intimidated by the size of the ever-growing crowd, announces through his interpreter, "At first, we will examine only the most seriously ill!"

"Bad move," I tell him as the throng surges forward, each patient perceiving their symptoms as qualifying them for immediate attention.

I explain to the students, "Any attempt to have the patients stratify themselves with respect to need just creates more confusion. The chronically ill elderly believe that their condition is most critical as they have been ill the longest, while the mother with an acutely ill child is aware that her child may not have long to live."

Dismayed, the student asks, "What can I do?"

The makeshift intensive care unit with volunteer medical students

I suggest, "During the course of the clinic, walk through the crowd searching for the ones you think have the most serious ailments."

Malaria season is in full swing, and many are very seriously ill. Periodically, a student meanders through the multitude searching for the most ill, while the other students start IVs on those who have severe malaria or are critically dehydrated.

Carol returns from the town and the crowd cheers, sings, and dances. She rolls up her sleeves and begins to assist with the treatments. A film crew from the United States arrives to record the lives of expatriates living in Africa. The crew is overwhelmed by the dissonant sounds: babies crying, patients moaning, the crowd murmuring and, on the fringes, an ever-present, expressive drumbeat as the Batwa sing and dance to their ancient rhythms. They ask how we deal with such suffering. Carol points out that, in spite of the clamor of desperation and cries of the distressed, a pervasive joy can be perceived. "It's difficult to capture on film, but this joy can be experienced when people are truly united in caring for one another."

I attempt to demonstrate the art of medicine to Josh. Several hundred anxious patients push in around us. Out of the corner of my eye, I notice a Mutwa furtively hiding behind a tree. Aware that he has been noticed, he quickly darts to another tree. I leave my workplace and slowly approach him. I tell him, "I am a physician and would like to help you." As he reluctantly inches forward, I am overwhelmed by the unmistakable smell of rotting flesh.

I introduce myself, and he then offers, "My name is Edson."

His features are hard to decipher. Sunken, frightened eyes gaze out from a tattered scarf encasing his head. Fetid rags wrap his left arm, and a torn oversized jacket hangs limply from hunched shoulders. Edson is short, even for a Mutwa. His gaze is fixed on the ground.

He timidly relates his trauma with the help of a translator, "I have a seizure and drop into an open fire. There is no one to pull me out. I walk to a government clinic for treatment but am turned away because I have no money." Without medical attention and no one to care for him, Edson lives alone, miserable and abandoned. There is little flesh remaining on his frame, I am surprised that he is still alive.

I introduce Edson to Josh, who agrees to assist in the treatment of this gaunt man. Cautiously and with great patience, Josh removes the rags. Edison has suffered deep, third-degree burns to his arm and chest. I instruct Josh in debridement, how to excise dead tissue:

"Surgery is simple, Josh. Just cut away the bad and leave the good. These burns have permanently damaged the nerves, so Edson cannot feel pain. You can cut away the dead tissue without anesthesia."

Josh's initial hesitancy is replaced with determination as he begins the ordeal of removing the rotten tissue. I return to the crowd of waiting patients.

Several minutes later, Josh comes over with a distraught look on his face, "Dad, Edson has worms."

On further inspection, Edson's burns do contain maggots. "Maggots are Edson's friends," I say. "They help cleanse the dead tissue. As a matter of fact, it was the therapy of choice in the distant past." Josh isn't impressed with my explanation but continues his work without complaint.

Later he asks me to examine Edson again. Josh taps on an area of white hard material in the center of the burn on Edson's arm, "What's that?"

"That's the radius. Edson's burn is so deep that it has destroyed all the tissue down to the bone."

After many hours of difficult debridement, Edson's arm is clean and respectable.

We give Edson everything that we have for his condition: a large supply of antibiotics, dressings, and money for food. We offer encouragement and a prayer and send him on his way.

As Edson departs, I explain to Josh, "Edson's prognosis is still very poor. He will probably need to have his arm amputated. He is unlikely to survive."

Josh responds, "Dad, Edson has lived this long with the infection. He's gotta be a tough guy."

I do not see Edson again for another year. While conducting a medical clinic at a remote Batwa settlement, a fellow approaches with a wide grin. It is Edson! Carol and I are delighted to see him. He proudly shows us his scarred, disfigured, but still-attached arm. His chest is healed. He seems happy, but we learn that he is still living an isolated life.

Carol tells Edson, "We will return soon, we would like to see you again."

We locate Edson several weeks later and Carol presents him with a Texas hat, a Texas longhorn shirt, and a sleeping mat.

Edson tries on the clothes as he looks at his reflection in our ambulance's mirror. His face is radiant.

"Now with my new clothes and sleeping mat, I will get married!"

I turn to Carol and chuckle, "Clothes might make the man, but is that all that it takes?"

Carol asks Edson about his marital plans.

A well-clad Edson

"I go to the Congo to find myself a pretty Mutwa woman and bring her back to live with me," he replies with great confidence.

Shortly thereafter, we are happy to donate a goat to celebrate the occasion of his betrothal at a gala party. Edson asks after Josh, saying, "He is the best doctor. I am sure that you are proud of him."

I have to agree with Edson; Josh provided fine surgical technique. More importantly, Josh dealt with the wounds of rejection and despair. Surgery and antibiotics were administered, but Josh's compassion was the key to healing. Edson's gratitude fully paid for our effort.

CHAPTER 10

✧ ✧ ✧

Father Fred's Redemption

"No hill without gravestones, no valley without shadows."
————— • West African Proverb • ——

Our mobile medical clinics reach only a small fraction of the Batwa population. We remain shocked and grieved by the persistence of sudden death among their children. It seems that there's a gossamer veil between this world and the next. Almost any disease, even minor ailments, can quickly bring death. The almost daily soulful beating of drums carries news of a recent death. Burials proceed quickly, as there is no access to embalming. Usually, the body is interred by the second day, but the memorial continues for an additional five to seven days.

We make a special effort to attend these burials to show respect for the recently departed and to comfort the family members. It is an occasion to get to know the Batwa better.

We are invited to attend the burial of a young Mutwa woman named Enid. She is the wife of Innocent, a musically talented Mutwa. A week earlier, Innocent had been given an American guitar to replace his homemade one. We were impressed by his old home-made guitar; although crudely constructed, it produced a fine sound. Innocent would serenade us with traditional Batwa songs, but he could also produce a fair rendition of Led Zeppelin's "Stairway to Heaven," as well as an occasional Jimi Hendrix riff. Innocent trea-sures his new guitar, playing it constantly, frequently jamming with

Enos. Where a week earlier there was singing and dancing, today there is weeping and mourning. A coffin for Enid is constructed on site, using two-foot-by-ten-foot boards. We donate the seven-dollar burial expense. Burials tend to be very social occasions; alcohol is liberally shared, adding to the festive spirit.

Father Fred, an Anglican pastor from a distant church, is summoned to officiate. Father Fred is dressed in his flowing priestly raiment; the Batwa wear rags. During the memorial, Father Fred, adding guilt to their misery, exhorts the Batwa to attend his Sunday service rather than party and drink *tonto* (a locally made banana wine).

Enid's mother stands to say a few words. Her wispy frame has been contorted from the daily toils of life. Her voice is as taut as one of Innocent's guitar strings. She hesitates frequently as she relates her story of motherhood: "I produce ten children, only two are alive."

The Batwa respond in unison "*Ka wa reeba,*" (Oh, what you experience).

Rain begins to fall, and we seek refuge under a banana tree. As the coffin is lowered into the pit, the deep mournful cries overwhelm my senses. On the hillside above me, women wail and rend their clothes; below, inebriated Batwa men joke among themselves as they shovel dirt into the grave. One particularly intoxicated digger falls into the pit and is unable to crawl out. Several other Batwa fail miserably as they attempt to rescue their friend. A few yards away, Father Fred and his staff huddle under colorful umbrellas, gustily singing Anglican hymns, oblivious to the drunken Mutwa flailing on the lid of the coffin.

After a closing prayer, Father Fred and his team hastily depart. I am startled by his insensitivity and failure to engage with the Batwa.

After the inebriated Mutwa is extricated from the grave and the last of the dirt is shoveled in, I ask a group of Batwa, "Do you believe that anything spiritual happens after death?"

I'm told, "At times, the evil spirit of *Nabingi* (Ná-Bin-gí – a minor god) is released from the dead and comes to disturb the living. *Nabingi* can cause a variety of diseases that can only be cured by the *abafumu* (Ah-Bá-fumu – traditional healers), using herbs obtained from the forest."

It seems that placating evil spirits is central to the Batwa's religious beliefs. The Batwa deny the existence of any good spirits emanating from the dead, but they believe there is a greater spirit, *Nagasan*, who came before all other spirits and is more powerful than *Nabingi*. They speak of *Nagasan* infrequently but with great reverence.

Mamia, our Mutwa friend, emphatically states, "It is *Nagasan* who gives us the forest, who is loving and compassionate, and who cares for the Batwa. *Nagasan* is our protector and sustainer."

Mamia motions me to follow her. Although her body is stooped with advanced arthritis, she easily negotiates a narrow winding trail. My eyes adjust to the dimming light as the jungle envelops us. Mamia knows the path well, traversing a twisted tree, ducking under a hanging vine. Grasping my hand, she leads me to an area surrounded by several enormous rocks.

She begins, "In the forest, when a Mutwa dies, we wrap the body with reeds just like this." She gathers a large clump of grass and binds it with vines to resemble a body. "While the body is being tied with vines, the villagers pack their few belongings and begin moving to another location in the forest." Staring at me through cloudy eyes, she adds, "We believe that *Nabingi* is angered when someone dies. We must quickly leave this spot or bad things will continue to happen."

Mamia then adjusts the bound grass into the posture of a body leaning on a boulder and finds two nuts to serve as eyes. "Before we depart, the dead body is placed into a sitting position, eyes open, looking upward. With eyes gazing upward, the dead cannot watch their family depart, but are able to scan the treetops searching for bees that might lead us to honey." She adds, "We Batwa love honey."

Mamia indicates that it is time to depart. As she does, tears mist her eyes. "Now the dead are placed in a box under the ground where there are no bees, no honey, no forest, only loneliness. This makes *Nagasan* and the Batwa very unhappy."

Mamia and I return to the burial. The rains have abated and a dense mist hangs over the nearby Bwindi Forest. The Batwa's spirits are now running high, the conversations are animated, food is distributed, banana wine flows, and the singing is gusty. Enid is remembered and celebrated.

A month after Enid's burial, Father Fred reemerges. We have transferred a pregnant Mutwa woman, Gladys, to a government hospital for delivery and Carol is attempting to call the hospital. Carol's frustration is obvious, as she is repetitively disconnected. The snippet of information that she obtains is concerning. Gladys requires a cesarian section to save the infant's life; however, the hospital's surgical theater's roof has collapsed. She must be transferred to another hospital, and our ambulance is the only one available.

Carol relates, "Gladys is Jeffrey's wife number three; the first two died in labor. Of his ten children, only three have survived. We must help."

Our day is already planned for a mobile medical clinic at the distant Batwa settlement. Carol suggests that she take our ambulance to transport Gladys to a functioning facility and that I locate a vehicle to drive to the mobile clinic. With a hug and kiss, Carol departs.

The clinic is busy, but my mind goes frequently to Carol. Will she be alright? I don't see her again until she returns just before dark. She's had a difficult day but is eager to share it.

I hand her a cup of steaming tea and her story begins: "I had not driven far from our home when a family with a very sick man requested a ride. I wanted to say 'No' as the car was already full of folks who needed a ride to town. Five more people piled in with their sleeping mats and supplies. The sick fellow was breathing with diffi-culty and so they placed him on one of the bench seats with his head in his wife's lap."

"Sounds like this trip will be another adventure," I comment.

"The adventure is not just the driving, but the stress; I felt alone and inadequate. I realized that the man's condition was worsening. With each of his labored breaths and cries from his loved ones, my hands tightened on the steering wheel. I asked God for strength and relaxed a little. After a short drive, who should I see standing in the middle of the road flagging me down but Pastor Fred."

Carol confesses, "I was angry at Pastor Fred! Didn't he know I was in a hurry? But it was either pick up Fred or run him down."

I nod, suppressing a laugh.

"After about fifteen minutes with Fred in the car, the patient's labored breathing ceases. I think, 'Wonderful, our patient has gone to sleep!' But then, from the rear of the vehicle comes a cry: 'He is dead!' I stop the car and the family takes the body out and puts it under a bush in the shade. His wife removes her scarf, tying it around her husband's jaw and nose." Carol asks, "Do they do this to keep the maggot flies out?"

"No sweetie, not for the maggots, but to close the mouth before rigor mortis sets in."

"That's better, I do not like the thought of maggots."

We sit for a while before Carol resumes. "The wife starts to dress him in a suit. She first has to remove some clothing, but she fumbles so much with the buttons, another man takes over. The shade under the bush is a mortuary, and my ambulance a hearse. There is much wailing. The dressed body is placed on the floor of our vehicle. Extra people pile in, and I head back the way I had come; this was not the way that my spirit wants to go."

I add, "This seems like a mission of mercy, but I was worried for you. I was praying that you were safe."

Carol continues, "I was worried too, but there was not much opportunity to consider myself. Along the way, as we slowed the car to spread the bad news, I heard screams of anguish and sobbing. When we arrived at the dead man's home, the sounds of mourning came from everywhere. The body was taken from the vehicle, and I followed everyone into a darkened room where the body was gently placed on a mat on the dirt floor. It was then that Pastor Fred's presence brought order out of chaos. He started singing and people joined in with voices raised, remembering something beyond them that is their rock and sure foundation."

I refill Carol's cup of tea and she takes a few sips before continuing. "Pastor Fred and I returned to the car. A relative wanted us to take the body to another location, thirty minutes round trip. Any other time, I would have gladly done so, but I said, 'No,' anxious about Gladys and her necessary transfer. The relatives kept pressing, but Pastor Fred came to the rescue. He told them, 'While this one has died, another might live.' All agreed. My attitude about Pastor Fred is changing, he was a godsend today!"

"I was very worried about Gladys and drove too fast for the conditions of the road. The vehicle was rattling loudly. My constant prayers were the glue that held the vehicle and me together. When I arrived, a nurse midwife told me that Gladys had already been transferred to another hospital by private vehicle. Her baby boy was delivered by Cesarean section. He had difficulty initially, but now he is breathing well."

Carol begins to weep.

As I comfort Carol, I murmur, "It must be a huge relief that the child has survived."

Carol responds, "I'm crying for relief, but also for joy. This day reminds me how arrogant I can be about the importance of my plans. God is in control; it's nice to see that confirmed."

CHAPTER 11

✤ ✤ ✤

An Injured Back and a Missing Key

*"When you carry your own water,
you will learn the value of every drop."*

——— ◆ African Proverb ◆ ———

Our mobile medical clinics are held at remote Batwa settlements. We work until the sun sets and frequently camp nearby. Carol and I, realizing that we need to improve our tent accommodations, have upgraded to a comfortable, four-inch foam mattress to assure a good night's sleep. The evening activities always include a period of stretches designed to limber up the back. In the mornings, we are greeted with birds chirping, colobus monkeys grunting, and my bones popping. I avoid doing a luxurious, cat-like stretch for fear that the muscles might seize up, leaving me compressed in a ball. Instead, I gingerly test the joints, my limits of mobility, and then slowly pull myself up and out of the tent. I am pleased whenever I can stand erect, relatively pain free. A lingering thought always haunts me: How long will these old bones tolerate Africa? My back has been acting up and visits to the pit latrine have become more of a challenge. I have nightmares that one day, the joints will freeze and, when I am finally discovered, my remains will still be poised over the long-drop pit, a grimace permanently etched on my skeletonized face.

Late one day, after returning from a medical clinic to our house adjacent to the bishop, while lifting a heavy, wet tent from our vehicle, I suddenly feel a lancinating lower back pain radiating down my right leg. My strength fails and I collapse on my knees. The pain is deep and searing. I realize that I've ruptured a disc. The next day, I have difficulty walking and the pain is excruciating. Lying in bed is painful, sitting is painful, and walking even a few feet is almost unbearable. It's equally concerning that I am unable to elevate my right big toe and that the top of my foot is numb. I rap on my knee and ankle with a reflex hammer and find the reflexes are intact. It becomes apparent that I have a serious neurological complication from a ruptured disc between the fourth and fifth lumbar vertebra, which may require corrective neurosurgery.

The nearest CT scanner is in Nairobi, a grueling three-day drive from the Bwindi. As I'm literally incapacitated, Carol must carry on alone. We are in a difficult situation.

Carol confides in me, "The possibility of leaving Uganda for you to seek back care makes me realize how much I love it here: the work, our spiritual growth, and our deepening relationship. I realize that if we are to stay, I will need to assume a larger role. Let's give it a try."

The next day, Carol anxiously prepares to drive to Kitariro, a Batwa settlement on the edge of the Bwindi Impenetrable Forest. The drive will be arduous and the work challenging. The Batwa of Kitariro reside in grass or mud huts, living in abject poverty. Accompanying Carol are Enos and Peace, the nurse we recently hired to work at the settlement. The purpose of their trip is to assess the feasibility of upgrading the current rudimentary medical clinic and to construct an adjoining house for Peace. A resident nurse will make a vast improvement in the Batwa's health. This project also includes building two latrines and remodeling a school. Carol reminds me that our schoolteacher currently teaches over sixty children in a ten-by-fifteen-foot thatched room with a mud floor, containing no desks, benches, blackboard, or books.

I bid her goodbye, and we pray that all goes well. Towards the end of the day, Carol returns from Kitariro bringing a cargo of sick Batwa and their relatives. It is obvious that it has been a long day. While the ambulance is being unloaded, Carol relates, "The roads here test all my driving skills, but I am pleased that no one died along the way."

"I know the road well. I bet that you relied on Divine guidance," I respond, while putting on a pot of tea and bringing out a few cookies.

Carol continues her saga: "Our prayers for a safe journey were heartfelt. We crawled along in our Land Rover ambulance in four-wheel-drive. Occasionally, the vehicle went sideways on the steep incline; the passengers screeched as they peered over a cliff. I consciously breathed out fear and breathed in God's peace, barely managing not to hyperventilate. My anxiety dissolved on arrival when I was greeted with drumming, song, and dance. Then, we discovered the future clinic was locked with no key available.

As I pour tea for everyone, I remark, "Locks are common, but keys are rare."

Carol mentions a close encounter with a pit latrine: "The Batwa were digging a pit latrine nearby. At sixteen feet deep, they hit rock, and every strike of the pick brought sparks. I approached to take a closer look and an elderly Mutwa woman suddenly grabbed me and pulled me back. It was only then that I noticed the old pit latrine lying in pieces nearby. I shuddered at the thought of anyone using it at the time it collapsed."

Carol indicates that her story will require another cup of tea. "It was getting late, and still, the man with the key to the clinic had not showed up. Suddenly, a young, excited Mutwa ran up to tell us that an elderly woman named Jacint was ill. We made our way down a steep slope to her simple hut. Inside was pitch-black darkness. I waited in vain for my eyes to adjust, and I followed the sounds of crying and groaning into the corner of the room. Jacint was lying on a straw mat, suffering, I guessed, from severe malaria. We all agreed she needed urgent medical care.

"Then, I was asked to see a sick young person next door. When I entered her house, she was shaking like a leaf. I think she also had malaria. We loaded those two patients into the ambulance, along with a few family members, and headed for home. Suddenly, the ambulance hit a large rock and, wham! It stopped. In my excited state, I couldn't find low range, but, after prayers, my hand got steadier, and the tractor gear clicked in. The differential was apparently undamaged. We continued as the passengers broke into joyful singing!"

As Carol finishes her engaging story, I look up in amazement to see all the Batwa Carol has brought back still silently fixated on us. They giggle as they see me rubbing Carol's back.

While not pain free, I have the wherewithal to examine the patients and administer the necessary medications. Conditions of the sick ones stabilize. After they do, I place a bar of precious chocolate onto a table in our living room. Carol asks the Batwa, "Have you ever eaten chocolate?" Two smell it and give their squares back. A third tastes the chocolate and is not pleased. A fourth licks it and, with a frown, places in into the discard pile.

Carol loads the Batwa into the ambulance returning them to their village. Believing that Carol surely is famished, I tell her our cook is preparing an African delicacy especially for her. She is exhausted when she returns from her second trip to Kitariro and joins me at the table with great expectations, yet her appetite suddenly vanishes when a platter of roasted grasshoppers is placed in front of her!

As we doze off, Carol reflects on what a relationship-building day it has been. Sleepily, she murmurs, "While the grasshoppers were not appetizing, a missing key and a locked door resulted in two lives being saved. When I am able to step out of my comfort zone and depend on God, good things happen. This gives me a sense of gratitude I wouldn't have anywhere else on earth."

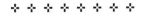

After six months, my back improves enough for me to make the trip to the U.S. for expert treatment. I schedule an appointment with a neurosurgeon to whom I've referred many patients when I was working in California. I am ushered into the exam room where MRI images of my back are displayed on a view-box. The surgeon enters the room looking dignified in his pressed white jacket, knotted tie, and carefully coiffed, gray hair. There is a computer clutched closely to his chest.

He's a very gifted surgeon but lacking in bedside manner. His personality is as cold as the surgical instruments that he ably wields. He asks me a few questions while he scans my MRI, typing my answers into the computer, never once looking at me. It reminds me of how I questioned the young woman years earlier. He then performs a cursory exam: rapping on my knee and Achilles tendon with a reflex hammer, poking my legs with a sharp instrument, and testing my legs for muscle strength. Satisfied with the exam and MRI report, he matter-of-factly states that my only hope for recovery is surgery.

"I will arrange for a decompression of your discs within a week," he states to his computer.

"Hold on a minute! Let's not be hasty with the scalpel," I plead.

Pointing to the MRI, he notes, "You will never be able to walk normally or hope to return to Africa without surgery. Just look at the size and location of this ruptured disc."

"I am aware of the MRI findings, and while I still can't raise my big toe and have some numbness, I feel great. In fact, I'm riding my bike and running up to five miles daily."

He disengages from the MRI. With a perplexed expression on his face, he looks at me and states, "That's impossible. It must be a miracle."

"I'll gladly accept a miracle; many folks have been praying for me."

I shake his hand, thank him for the advice, and hastily exit the office.

CHAPTER 12

✧ ✧ ✧

A Geography Lesson

"If you think education is expensive,
try ignorance."

———— ◆ African Proverb ◆ ————

The Batwa are achingly poor. They have few possessions and consume all that they can grow. Carol and I understand that providing for all their needs will do more harm than good. Giving them an education, however, could have a lasting positive impact. One definition of poverty is "a lack of options"; without an education, options are very limited.

The Batwa children rarely complete primary school. They are unable to pay school fees, buy supplies, or buy school clothes. Complicating the picture, families depend on every member's effort to provide food. When we ask the children why they are not in school, the most frequent answer is, "How can we study when our stomachs are empty?"

When we initially came to Uganda, no Batwa in the area had an education beyond the primary level. Carol is convinced that education and materials for learning must be without cost to them. We find that our initial forays into providing education are bearing fruit. The nursery and primary schools we support are expanding and we are scrambling to build additional furniture and hire more teachers. It is a good sign.

Then, we have a remarkable visit from Phyllis Atha, an artist from our community of Nevada County, California. She's come to volunteer. We are concerned about Phyllis's stay because we wonder how an artist will adapt to working with the Batwa. We are also alarmed when she informs us, "My life and diet are very organized and regimented. I'll require something similar in Africa."

Carol responds to Phyllis in an email: "Even the best-laid plans frequently go awry. We eat what food is available and sleep when the work is done. Typically, in order to prepare a meal, I shop at a few roadside stalls, each selling meager supplies. One stall may have a few tomatoes, another several eggs, and yet another a melon. For our rare chicken dinners, I negotiate a price for the scrawny thing, wring its neck, pluck the feathers, and gut it. I then make a fire and grill it. This process is exceedingly unlikely after a long day at a Batwa village. More often we eat what we have on hand—eggs, fruit, and peanut butter—and then fall into bed, exhausted."

Phyllis isn't pleased with our schedule or diet, but she agrees to come. Carol has an inspiration; she asks Phyllis to paint a map of the world on the wall of a classroom that we are remodeling. Phyllis duly arrives with several laminated maps for models. Thoughtfully, she brings tints that can be mixed with interior wall paint and an array of brushes. Most importantly, she brings a lively disposition.

When we visit the school, at first, Carol and Phyllis are simply entertainment for everyone. Then, Phyllis gets to work. She draws an outline of a map of the world on the front wall of the classroom, delineating all the countries. The Batwa pack the rear of the room, watching the map unfold. Phyllis discovers a young Mutwa woman named Abias who has a good sense of color. Abias makes everyone laugh with her wry comments.

While nursing her infant, Abias paints a few countries using a variety of colors. She then ascends a ladder to paint the upper right portion of the map. When she is finished with that region of the world, she drags the ladder over to the far-left side. Pointing to the upper segment, she asks, "What color should I use for this country?"

"The same color that you used for the upper right country," Phyllis responds.

Abias seems confused and walks over to talk with her Batwa friends. After an animated discussion, she approaches Phyllis with a curious look on her face, "Do I use the same color because this is the same country?"

"Yes, it is all one continuous country. Russia is its name," Phyllis confirms.

Abias again retreats to talk with the Batwa. The tenor of their conversation becomes excited, reaching a crescendo. Surging forth, the Batwa surround Phyllis and Carol. Filled with wonder, they ask, "If this is the same country, do you mean that the world is ROUND like an *amozi* (pumpkin)?"

When the response is affirmative, the room becomes electric.

The Batwa excitedly shout questions over one another:

"If the world is round, then what is on the inside?"

"What is on the outside?"

"We want to know these things!"

"Teach us!"

The Batwa's enthusiasm results in the creation of an adult education program. We restructure our schools so that the kids attend until mid-afternoon; afterward, adults fill the classrooms, eager to learn about their world.

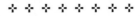

The map continues to be a source of interest and amazement to the Batwa. Groups of all ages spend hours poring over the map, discussing it with excitement. They ask questions about other cultures and other people.

"Look at the countries surrounding Uganda."

"Oh, the world is so large."

"We are all connected."

They ask Carol, "How do you travel to Africa?" She points to our hometown, Nevada City, California, where it is tucked in near the bend where Lake Tahoe touches Nevada. She then traces our airplane flight to London, then Nairobi, and finally Entebbe, Uganda.

"You fly on a *nyonyi* (big bird)?"

Carol says, "It's a very large metal bird. Flying is easy; the most difficult part of the trip is the sixteen-hour bus ride from the airport at Entebbe to the Bwindi."

The Batwa are amazed at the distances. "You came all this way to be with us!"

Another portion of the map confuses them. "What is all the blue?" Carol describes an ocean. It proves difficult for the Batwa to grasp, as their only frame of reference for a body of water is a stream or a pond.

Others are interested in the people that live in the United States.

They ask, "Do Africans live in America?"

Carol responds, "There are many Africans in the U.S."

"Where do they live?" the Batwa want to know.

"They live all over, in cities and in the countryside," Carol replies.

"What tribe do they belong to?"

Taking a deep breath, Carol tells them, "Most African Americans do not have tribal roots."

"Without a tribe to support them and help raise their children, how do they survive?" they ask. They are confused.

After reflecting for a moment, Carol explains, "In America, we have families, friends, our church and community organizations; we consider these people our tribe. Scott and I have parted from our family and friends in the U.S. to come live with you. You are our new tribe."

The Batwa smile with understanding. A simple lesson in geography not only expands their knowledge of the world but also fosters an understanding that we all are united as neighbors.

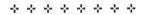

The Batwa are exceedingly creative in providing for themselves and it's obvious that a traditional education does not fully utilize their talents. A few flourish in school, but many do not last, eventually dropping out. An expanded array of educational options is required to allow the Batwa to become self-sufficient.

Perhaps as proof that God works in mysterious ways, an act of stealing alters our approach to education. Carol realizes that money has been taken from her purse. The Batwa find two of their young men who confess to the crime. One regrets only that he's been caught, but the other, Timothee, says he's truly sorry, will never do it again, and asks for forgiveness.

Carol sits with Timothee and inquires, "Why would you steal from me? Why didn't you ask me for help?"

Timothee hangs his head in shame. "I have no money for food, salt, sugar, soap, or a bucket for washing. I work in a field owned by the Bakiga. I'm paid with a small part of what I harvest or I'm given one meal for a day's labor. It is barely enough to keep me alive."

His sense of hopelessness strikes Carol. She is convinced that Timothee wants to work so that he can achieve a sense of dignity and buy basic necessities without having to beg or steal. Carol decides to initiate a vocational program, starting with masonry.

We tap on our friends in the U.S. who eagerly support such a program and Carol hires a mason to teach the Batwa. We purchase tools, sand, cement, and bricks and decide to offer lunch during the days the masonry students will be away from their fields. The students begin constructing practice walls. The nurses' house needs some remodeling, so the mason and his students do the work. A pit latrine structure is required; they build it. Next, they upgrade the nursery school. Timothee's talents are recognized, and he becomes the mason's assistant. He has a new confidence and tells Carol, "I will make three thousand Ugandan shillings ($1.25) a day as a mason. I will never beg or steal again!"

Several months later, when visiting a vocational program, we see the Batwa busily making furniture. Several Batwa carpenters approach Carol, saying, "Thank you! We now provide for our families." Carol and I walk to a quiet place overlooking the Bwindi.

Timothee in front of a wall he has constructed after being trained as a mason

I note, "All because of Timothee's confession, there are vocational training programs. You must be proud of what's been accomplished."

Carol is reflective. "He learned about personal integrity, and I learned about opening my heart to another. And besides, our rickety house furniture has been upgraded and holes in the walls are sealed—no more rats!"

CHAPTER 13

✣ ✣ ✣

Springs of Living Water

*"The usefulness of a well
is known when it dries up."*

——— • African Proverb • ———

Although we are living adjacent to a rain forest where pure rainwater falls in abundance, only 35 percent of people in this area have access to potable water and sanitation. At our mobile medical clinics, I find entirely too many diarrheal ailments. The most vulnerable? Children under age five.

A young boy named Innocent is an example. His mother carries him into our medical outreach, exhausted after a daylong hike from a remote village. Profuse diarrhea and vomiting for the past three days have given him pale, sunken eyes along with ribs and bones wrapped in loose coverings of skin. Excessive dehydration has collapsed his veins. I locate a vein and pump in IV fluids. With a few hours of intensive rehydration, his tissues fill and he becomes animated. Innocent continues to improve over the next few hours, tolerating oral fluids and gaining strength. I tell his mother that I am cautiously hopeful that he will survive. But in a few hours, Innocent's breathing slows, and his life slips away. His mother thanks me. She silently lifts her son, wraps him in her shawl, and, stooped by sorrow and the weight of her dead child, begins the lonely walk home.

Providing clean water will greatly improve the Batwa's health. Tom Myers and Brian Slattery, two young American engineers from our hometown, have learned about the need and have come to stay with us. Tom and Brian are energetic and enthusiastic about engaging with the Batwa. The Batwa settlement of Byumba has been ravaged by diarrheal illnesses and is in need of clean water. We had contacted several NGOs for assistance but were told that providing clean water requires drilling a borehole. The cost, a startling $5,000 to $10,000.

Clean water for the Batwa with Tom and Brian

Arriving at Byumba, Carol, Tom, Brian, and I pitch our tents on a high ridge overlooking the Bwindi Forest. As soon as we enter the Batwa village, Tom pulls a soccer ball from his backpack, twirls it on his index finger, and performs several acrobatic tricks to the cheers of the dazzled Batwa. A rock star is born. Tom and Brian quickly assess the situation and agree on a simple but unique plan. They tell us, "If the water is captured at its source and piped to a holding tank, it should work. But, the Batwa will have to help; a lot of effort is required."

I explain the plan to the Batwa, and they eagerly agree. They begin by carrying the gravel down to the site at the bottom of the valley. The hill is very steep, and no wheelbarrows are available, so they use makeshift buckets balanced on heads. A young girl, no older than three and no higher than our kneecaps, catches our attention. She carries a small bowl holding about three handfuls of gravel perched on her head, steadying the load with both hands. She is oblivious of us, casually making her way to the construction site. Brian steps up to the little girl with the thought of obtaining a photo. The young girl freezes, her face etched with horror, having never seen a *muzungu* before. She breaks into tears, but never lets her precious payload slip from her head.

Young and old pitch in to do the work. The intense labor is just another day to them. While the Batwa give themselves totally to the project, they are quiet and shy with outsiders until a relationship has been developed. As the project continues, the previously traumatized little girl opens up to the strange *bazungu*, smiling at Brian each time she passes, eventually running to him with her arms spread, eager to be held.

Brian with Batwa child

Today, the village is alive with purpose and comradery. Brian and Tom are knee deep in mud, surrounded by a dozen Batwa, all working as a team. Sitting on a nearby slope is a contingent of children singing and drumming, entertaining the workers. Every so often, the diggers encounter a nest of safari ants, which sends them into frenzied, painful contortions, producing howls of laughter from the children.

During a break from the work, Brian shares with me his thoughts on the Batwa: "When you invited Tom and me to help the Batwa, I thought that we would be doing the work for them. I had no idea that this would be a community project. It certainly made it more fun. These folks who have so little, but give so much, sharing their energy, smiles, and laughter. When one has nothing, love can still be given."

Carol adds, "It's a lesson that we have learned many times over, that in giving, we have received much from the Batwa."

Nestled in our tent that night, Carol and I talk about the success of the water project and how important it is to the health of the Batwa. The joy of our work is spilling over into our marriage.

I ask, "Do you think that the key to couples finding their marriages in need of a spark should just be selling their possessions and living in a tent?"

Carol smiles. "I don't think this approach will threaten the jobs of marriage counselors, but it's certainly working for us!"

Carol and Scott

CHAPTER 14

✢ ✢ ✢

Being Faithful

"When elephants fight, it's the grass that suffers."
—— • African Proverb • ——

Although Carol's and my communication has improved, our ability to connect this small patch of Africa with the world beyond remains challenging. There are no televisions, newspapers are rare, and accessing the internet is difficult. Our mail comes to a post office that's a two-hour drive from our house. We are able to use our phone and an internet signal only when we perch on top of a hill affording a line of sight to a cell tower. We live isolated from the outside world.

One evening, Carol and I drive to a high projection of rock to access our email. The connection to the cell tower is exceptionally poor, but we are able to download several emails. We find one email with a large attachment. The download is painfully slow. As the horizon darkens, we stand outside gazing at our computer resting on the hood of our Land Rover. Kerosene lamps and candles twinkle in the village below and the mosquitoes buzz about. A slice of a picture appears, revealing brown hair and,

Seth and Tera with our
first grandchild Lena

slowly, a portion of a forehead. Carol exclaims, "I'd recognize our son Seth anywhere." The next part of the picture reveals another face, "It's Tara! And look at that beaming smile."

As the picture progresses, we see that she is cradling a newborn. Carol shouts, "Our first grandchild!" We embrace and cry joyful tears.

Missing the birth of a grandchild isn't the only thing we've given up. Several days later, we make a lengthy trek to the post office to retrieve our mail and are surprised to receive a care package from Bob Lowe, a physician friend from our hometown. On the return trip, Carol tears into the package, finding precious items unavailable in Uganda.

Carol gleefully eyes our treasures, "Cheetos, granola, and chocolate, a complete meal!" She rips open a bag of Cheetos and hands me a few.

"There must be a problem; the Cheetos are stale. Cheetos never go stale."

Carol rips open another bag and grimaces, "So is the granola. Hard and dry."

Carol then reads the enclosed letter from Bob. "Those family events happened a while ago."

Carol passes a few photos by me. "The photos of the kids look pretty old," I remark. "When was the package sent?"

Carol lets out a hoot, "The package was mailed two-and-a-half years ago!"

Other correspondence is not so humorous and has ominous consequences for our work in Uganda. We receive information that the Episcopal Diocese of New Hampshire has elected a gay bishop, triggering a rift within the Episcopal Church. The Ugandan church has serious issues with the choice.

Carol asks, "What do you think will happen?"

I say, "Trouble's brewing. I fear this will end badly."

Six months later, a young, well-dressed teenager knocks on our door, hands me an official letter from the Archbishop of Uganda, and quickly departs. Carol and I are surprised by the formality of the delivery.

Carol attempts humor, "Perhaps an invitation to a gala celebration?"

We open the letter, and our faces fall when we read, "Because of the controversy in the church, you are immediately required to sever your ties with the Domestic and Foreign Mission Society of the Episcopal Church."

We are shocked by the news. These are our friends and supporters.

"This is harsh! This isn't a request, it's a demand. We can either stay and obey these orders or go home." As cradle Episcopalians, these are hard ties to break.

After some back and forth, we come to realize that our calling is spiritual and didn't come from the Mission Society. With great reluctance, we sever our ties with the Mission Society.

More difficulties occur. One of our volunteers criticizes a local NGO because they have been using donations for personal enrichment. The volunteer returns home but leaves trouble in his wake. The NGO drags me before Ugandan government officials and church leaders who threaten to have our visa revoked. During the inquest, it's apparent that the practice of "embezzlement" is commonplace, accepted by both church and state. Duly admonished, but retaining our visa, we learn yet another lesson in humility.

After dinner, we sit on the porch in the cool of the African evening and reflect on our recent problems. We realize how fragile and precarious our operations in Uganda are; our work could be brought to an immediate halt by the whim of either the church or the government, neither of whom seem supportive.

Albert Schweitzer once said, "Sometimes our light goes out, but is blown into flame by another human being. Each of us owes deepest gratitude to those who have rekindled this light." A spark comes to reawaken our downtrodden spirits in the form of an older American couple, seasoned missionaries, who are visiting the Bwindi to trek the gorillas. We invite them to dinner. They have accumulated much wisdom from their decades in Africa. Their hair has whitened and their tanned skin has wrinkled, but their ardor has not been dampened by the immense challenges of life in South Sudan. They are energetic and their eyes glitter with excitement. Gently holding hands, their demeanor reflects a deep love for each other.

Over a dinner of tough chicken, a few scraps of limp vegetables, and a mound of rice and matoke, the husband asks, "How are you doing?"

Thinking that he honestly wants to know, we pour out our concerns, "We enjoy our relationships with the Batwa, but the rift in the Episcopal Church has threatened our stay. In addition, we have recently had serious run-ins with the Ugandan authorities who seem not to support our projects. We feel our work here could end suddenly. We feel lost and are dispirited."

He pauses for a while to digest what we have said. "You clearly have a heart for these people and seem to resonate with them. You care for them very deeply." His eyes dance as he continues, "Do you think your mission is to be *successful* in your projects or is it to be *faithful* to your call?"

Successful versus faithful? The distinction strikes us like a thunderbolt as tears well up.

After a long pause, Carol says, "We feel like our hearts are drawn to the Batwa and we came with no set goals. We just wanted to help, but we measured our accomplishments by Western standards."

He persists, "Simplify your life, let the projects go. Just commit to improving your connections with the Batwa assuming that whatever comes out of those relationships will be valuable."

Carol laughs. "You mean discarding our expectations and giving ourselves the gift of living in the moment, just like the Batwa?"

"Just like the Batwa."

Our spark is reignited!

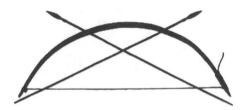

PART III (2003 – 2010)

Hope

"Hope Does Not Disappoint."
—— • South African Proverb • ——

"The hand that gives, also receives in return."
—— • East African Proverb • ——

CHAPTER 15

✛ ✛ ✛

New Hope

"If you dream of moving mountains tomorrow,
you must start by lifting small stones today."

——— · African Proverb · ———

O ver the years, our relationship with the Batwa flourishes. We sing and dance together and share many meals. They are teaching us about living in the moment. However, there is not much movement towards changes that can make a permanent difference in their lives. Our medical outreach is meager, still consisting almost entirely in the various mobile clinics we have been holding below ficus trees. It's a Band-Aid approach at best. Our trips taking sick Batwa to distant hospitals have made them aware of other options for medical care. They suggest that we consider building a clinic where regular and continuous care can be provided.

The neediest area in the region is a remote village named Buhoma, near the Bwindi Forest. The mobile clinics at Buhoma have proven to be the best attended and most critical. We typically treat three hundred to five hundred patients per day there. The elders in this community suggest a piece of land that might be available. When I walk the four-acre site, it seems a perfect location for a medical structure. A permanent clinic could be constructed on the flat, lower section of the land with staff houses positioned on the upper portion, affording both privacy and views of the Bwindi Impenetrable Forest.

While the elders have chosen good land, we lack adequate funds. As I begin negotiations with the owners of the property, it is apparent that they assume the "rich Americans" can afford to pay an exorbitant sum. Their initial asking price is $3,000, but they raise the price, and keep raising it exponentially. The initial cost doubles, then triples, and eventually increases eightfold.

Carol teases me, "Your negotiation skills might need some fine tuning."

Previously, when we had discussed with several NGOs the possibility of building a medical clinic, they were not encouraging. They bluntly told us that even if the construction of the clinic was possible, running the institution would be very difficult and should not be undertaken without significant funding and administrative skill. We didn't have either of those. They neglected to mention that acquiring the land would be just as problematic.

In the midst of the negotiations, we receive a visit from Bob and Pam Macauley, friends from the U.S. who are working in northern

Pam and Bob

Uganda. Bob is a pediatrician and Pam is a videographer who has previously worked for Oprah Winfrey. They are an intelligent and loving couple. Pam is pregnant with their first child. They are interested in medical outreach, and we arrange a trip to Buhoma for another mobile clinic.

When we arrive, we find a multitude of patients, including some incredibly ill young children, jammed together under the shade of the spreading ficus tree. Mothers stream forward cradling their infants while Pam captures it on video.

A mother, who has walked many hours through the forest, hands Bob her frail, two-year-old child. The child hangs limply in Bob's arms, her eyes totally vacant. A sudden thrashing begins as her delicate body contorts with a seizure. Bob quickly lays the child on the mother's lap and searches for a vein. No veins are visible. Bob places the child head down, and he is able to slither a catheter into an obscure neck vein. Intravenous fluids and medications for the seizures and malaria are administered. The mother comforts her child in her willowy arms as the seizures cease and breathing normalizes.

We alternate two-hour shifts throughout the night, monitoring the child's progress and administering the intravenous medications. Before dawn breaks, the child's raspy breathing is irregular and labored.

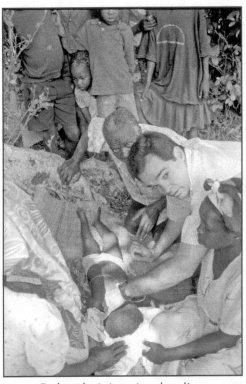

Bob administering healing

With a final gasp, her chest expands no more. Hope disappears from the mother's eyes. We are deeply saddened for her and her little girl. As both Bob and I are familiar with what the child needed and know how easily it might have been provided in a hospital with resources, we are aware that this is another unnecessary death.

We find ourselves exhausted, yet the clinic is scheduled to extend another day. We pray that we will have the resolve to assist the sick. We read in Romans 12:12, "Rejoice in hope, be patient in tribulation, and constant in prayer." We return to the ficus tree and are again surrounded by patients. Hope is in short supply and our patience is tested; still, the verse is a promise and a gift from God in the midst of what we face.

Then, a surprise. My friend Elphaz, a community elder, approaches me. I have known Elphaz for years. Although elderly, his skin is smooth, his vision unclouded by cataracts, and his hearty laugh and broad grin reveal teeth not discolored by time. Simply dressed in a frayed white shirt and dark pants, he exudes confidence. He is a man who has taken care of himself and others over his lifetime and has not given in to the frailties of aging. He is respected as a village leader and his opinion is highly valued. He's typically addressed as "Chief." Elphaz tells me that the council of elders wants to talk with me. Bob agrees to handle the medical clinic, and Carol and I accompany Elphaz to an assembly of nine elders congregated in a tight circle. The owners of the property are also present.

Elphaz addresses us: "We have gathered to discuss the land acquisition for the permanent clinic. We all agree that this land is the best place for a clinic. It is one of the few flat properties in this mountainous region. We are also aware that the price is too high." Elphaz turns to Carol and me and asks, "May we elders be allowed to talk with the owners to find out if there can be a compromise?"

I've been so frustrated by my own negotiations, I tell them, "Please do discuss the land, but I would rather not be involved. In case you need help, Carol and I will remain nearby. If you have any questions, we'll be available."

Carol agrees, "I think that our best contribution is silence."

Carol and I sit on a rock and gather our thoughts. We are aware that this is the neediest area in the region and there are no medical services within hours of driving. This land is centrally located and an easy walk for the Batwa. However, our funds are nearly depleted; we have only $3,000 remaining in our account.

We listen intently to the animated and heated debate between elders and owners. By the intensity and tenor of the discussions, I am aware that an impasse has developed. Suddenly, the shouting comes to an abrupt halt and a long silence ensues. Gradually, a very reserved conversation resumes. When the discussions conclude, the elders approach and sit with us.

They ask, "Will you be willing to pay $3,000 for the property?"

Carol and I are shocked, "How did you do it? We tried hard to negotiate such a price."

An elder relates the conversation: "Initially, the talks were very divisive, focusing solely on money. We passionately argued back and forth about the price, without much success. Chief Elphaz interrupted us with a command: 'All quarrelling must cease!' He then asked, 'What is the purpose of these negotiations?' The elders and property owners agreed that the intention was to acquire land to build a medical clinic. Elphaz then asked, 'Why is this clinic necessary?' We all answered, 'The clinic is necessary to prevent the deaths of our young children.' No one spoke for a long time; each one of us was remembering with sorrow the deaths of our own children. Then we agreed that $3,000 is a reasonable amount for the property."

The elders sit next to us and enquire, "Since we are willing to offer you this land, will you heal the diseases afflicting our community? Will you provide care for our children as well?"

I thank them for allowing us to purchase the land, and I tell them, "I believe that we will be able to save your children's lives, but only if we work together."

All laugh when I add, "Perhaps you can also teach me how to negotiate."

It is apparent that we have all been made richer by this act of giving. We sign the land agreement amid joyous singing and dancing.

Before departing, Chief Elphaz remarks, "Now the hard work begins."

Later that night, Carol and I sit together on the porch, listening to the evening forest creatures. I ask Carol if she remembers Bethany Norman's visit several years ago. Bethany was a volunteer from Nevada City. At a mobile medical clinic, we were asked to assist a woman in labor. It was an exceedingly difficult home delivery; at birth, the infant was not breathing. We tried in vain to resuscitate the child, but she died in Bethany's arms. We returned the following day for the burial and watched men cut wood for the coffin.

Carol sadly laments, "I can never forget that day, particularly Bethany's comment when the coffin was lowered into the ground. 'Coffins should not be that small,' she said."

I remember the countless burials of young children we have attended. As the Batwa say, "The coffin is small, but it is the heaviest to carry."

With a hopeful spirit, Carol notes, "The mobile medical clinic under the spreading ficus tree will be replaced by a permanent structure. Infant deaths will be prevented. Tribulation will be exchanged for hope."

CHAPTER 16

✤ ✤ ✤

Ant Attack

"Ants united can carry a dead elephant to their cave."

—— • African Proverb • ——

As Carol and I get to know the Batwa better, they come to trust us and allow us into their lives. One of my great pleasures is hiking with the Batwa, attempting to see the Bwindi through their eyes. Their ability to travel through a rain forest is phenomenal. Studies indicate that the Batwa's bone and joint structure allows them to move in a far more fluid fashion through dense undergrowth than other tribal groups, especially this *muzungu*. I exercise daily in an effort to keep pace with the Batwa, but on trips through the jungle, they far outstrip me. My language skills have improved enough so I can recognize that many of their comments about me are not very complimentary: "Why is the *muzungu* perspiring profusely and gasping for breath? He's not even carrying anything!"

An endless web of trails weave through the brilliant foliage of the Bwindi Forest. We stop periodically to relax. As I catch my breath, my thoughts tend to turn inward, while the Batwa remain ever vigilant. I feel a tap on my shoulder with "*Reeba,*" (Reä—bá—look), and my attention is directed to a bird with brilliant plumage perched high in the canopy. Then another tap, "*Enkima,*" (En-Chi—má—monkey), while they point to a white-faced Colobus monkey sitting motionless on a distant branch.

Other creatures are not so easy to overlook. On a hiking trip with my friend James, I am not paying attention. James suddenly grabs my arm, "*Reeka, hati!*" (Stop, now!). I notice the bushes gently swaying next to us. Suddenly, a huge silverback gorilla emerges from the underbrush accompanied by several smaller gorillas. The silverback stands upright, pounding his huge chest. I feel the urge to run and my heart races; however, James remains motionless, staring intently at the gorilla. The silverback emits a menacing growl and charges, but abruptly halts a few feet away, apparently realizing that we are not a threat. The silverback turns, and, following his troupe, saunters off, quickly vanishing into the forest. James's grip on my arm lessens and my breathing and heart rate eventually normalize.

"*Natiina,*" (I am afraid), I blurt out.

James calmly says, "These gorillas are our friends; we share the forest with them. They will not harm you. Don't fear. Fear prevents you from understanding the forest."

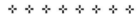

Above the land that we have purchased for the future clinic, we construct a three-bedroom guest house. One bedroom is for males, another for females, and the third is a cozy room for Carol and me. A kitchen, bathroom, shower, and dining area complete the communal living structure. The evenings are never dull as the students talk over the events of the day long into the night, often lamenting the difficulties of medical practice without the amenities of diagnostic equipment available in the U.S. More problematic for a good night's rest is that several students are attracted to African drumming.

We soon realize that privacy and sleep are essential. We purchase a nearby plot of land that is directly adjacent to the Bwindi and build a simple dwelling constructed of logs interlaid with masonry. It is functional and very romantic. No other structures are in sight, and our only neighbors are monkeys and birds. From the porch, we can

View from Carol and Scott's home

peer directly into the forest canopy, where our artist friend Phyllis noticed twenty-three different shades of green.

Our cabinets are sealed to prevent baboon raids. A simple, open shower sits at one corner of the porch, affording a grand vista of the park. While Carol is showering, occasionally she has the haunting feeling that she is being watched, only to look up and see a curious monkey perched a few feet above, following her every move.

We awaken to the howls of monkeys and the chirping of birds. The forest is alive. The only time it seems to sleep is between two and four o'clock in the morning. When I return from an emergency and sit on my porch at this early hour, there is an enveloping peace before the coming of the dawn.

Our new cabin is a wonderful retreat for the night, but we continue to share all our meals with the students at the clinic's guest house; this is where we all learn from one another and enjoy lively conversation. Over dinner, one of the visiting medical students asks about the ants that he has seen. I mention that elephants may be the biggest land animals, and gorillas the largest primates, but ants are the real kings. "You've seen the safari ants. They stream along in a very organized fashion. The worker ants flow like rivers, with the soldiers taking up a defensive position along the perimeter. Soldier ants are exceedingly large, sterile females, approximately one inch in length, with bulbous heads sporting snapping pincers."

Another student chimes in, "I have read that these ants are called suture ants. Why is that?"

I relate that some of the traditional healers who live in remote areas have told me that they use the ants to repair wounds. If the skin is accidentally cut, the edges of the laceration are aligned and a few suture ants applied, their pincers snap along the wound margins. The body of the ant is then broken off and the head will remain attached for several days. Fresh ants can be applied until the wound heals.

I conclude with the admonition, "The only time to truly worry about the ants is when food becomes scarce. Then, the safari ants will forage. They fan out into a wide undulating mass, moving at sixty feet per hour, consuming everything in their path."

Several of the students shudder at this thought.

A few weeks later, Sarah, a young pre-med volunteer with curly blond hair, learns the hard way about the ants' tenacity. Late one day, as we are descending the narrow winding path from the guest house to attend to a medical emergency at the clinic, a few bites on my legs get my immediate attention.

I tell Sarah, "Hurry up; the ants are swarming around us!"

In her excitement, Sarah slips and falls into the seething mass. I quickly pull her out, but not before a host of ants become ensnared in her flowing hair. She screeches, running back to the guest house where she is assisted by staff who help extract the ants. It would be an understatement to say that she was unhappy. "The event will remain one of my worst nightmares," she says.

After dinner that evening, Carol and I retire to our house. While lighting our kerosene lanterns, I hear what sounds like raindrops. This seems odd, as it is a star-filled, cloudless sky. As I stand by our bed, I feel something crawl up my leg. I brush it off but, *ouch*, a substantial bite quickly focuses my attention. I light a kerosene lantern to identify the culprit but see nothing in the dim light. All of a sudden, I feel a mob of bugs on my legs and receive multiple searingly painful bites. I hop onto the bed and look down. The floor is a swirling sea of safari ants invading our premises.

I am somewhat fascinated but mostly alarmed. I alert Carol, "We're having an ant attack!"

I watch a large earwig twisting and turning due to a sizable suture ant whose jaws are firmly attached to its snout. The battle is quickly over with the earwig motionless, its great tail pincher rendered useless.

Carol quickly tosses me our trusty can of "Doom" insecticide, saying, "This'll take care of them."

The deadly spray is quickly exhausted. Carol, pointing at the undulating mass of ants pouring out between the floorboards, shouts, "We are the *doomed* ones!"

She tilts the lantern to cast light on the far wall. It is covered with ants. "We are living a horror movie! Let's get outta here!"

We quickly flee the advancing army and race to our Land Rover. We are accompanied on our flight by insects, lizards, and a multitude of other creatures.

As we depart, I tell Carol, "Do you remember the sound of raindrops that I heard earlier? It was the clatter of these critters striking our house in their frantic attempt to escape the ants."

When we return the next morning, we find that all food not placed in a sealed container has been devoured. The area next to the bed where we had sprayed "Doom" has been covered with dirt carried in by the ants to protect against further casualties. All their fallen comrades have been removed. No Ant Left Behind.

"Well, our problem with rats has been solved," as Carol pokes at several carcasses stripped to the bone.

I remind Carol of a quote from Proverbs, "Go to the ant, thou sluggard; consider her ways and become wise." She gives me a look, and I ponder the wisdom other proverbs counsel about keeping silence.

As Carol is sweeping the last remains of the invasion out the door, she comments, "I'm none the wiser, but I do have a greater appreciation of our relationship with ants in *their* food chain."

CHAPTER 17

✤ ✤ ✤

Land and Health

"The earth is not ours,

it's a treasure that we hold for future generations."

—— · African Proverb · ——

I continue to worry about what it will take to build and launch a medical clinic. Carol's conversations with the Batwa sends her thinking in another direction. Sipping tea one night with several medical students on the porch of the guest house, Carol challenges the students, "You've been talking at length about the treatment of a variety of tropical diseases—this is your training. But isn't it also your job to prevent these people from getting sick?"

A lively discussion follows regarding preventive medicine and public health, including clean water, malaria prevention, and improved diets.

One student asks, "What are the major determinants of ill health among the Batwa?"

Carol departs for a few minutes and returns carrying a large binder containing recent studies on Batwa health compiled by a Tulane public health student, Colleen D'Aquin. Carol flips through a few pages, finding a relevant statistic: "Under age five, mortality is 59 percent among the landless Batwa, but if they own land, it drops to 38 percent. Just owning land reduces mortality by a third."

A student adds, "I wish that it were so easy in the U.S. Why is land ownership such an issue?"

Carol tells the students, "The Bakiga own most of the land. It is only sold in desperate circumstances and usually to friends or family members, not to the Batwa."

I explain that when we visit the Batwa, they tell us stories of desperate circumstances. Many survive as squatters living on land owned by the Bakiga. They are required to give the owner one-half of what they grow. There is a lack of clean water, sanitation, and adequate housing.

Carol puts her arm in mine. "It's fine to have a hospital, but don't you think that purchasing land for the Batwa is also a high priority?"

I whisper, "Great idea, but please remember that we have no money."

Carol continues, "Land is of primary importance to the Batwa's survival."

Caught up in the spirit of the moment, she says, "Let's begin with helping our friend Flora!"

Flora is a diminutive, elderly female and the matriarch of six landless families residing nearby. For years, she has had a draining area on the side of her neck, which we found was due to tuberculosis. After treatment, she is left with a large, dimpled scar. We've been good friends since I treated her.

Flora is always smiling, and she's a marvelous storyteller. She recounts meeting her future husband: "We meet in the forest while he is on a hunt. It is a rainy day, and I am living under a large tree. I am chilled and he helps me build a fire."

With a cute grin, she says, "He keeps me very warm."

One of Flora's daughters was born deaf and is unable to speak. Flora takes special care of this child. We desperately want to help Flora and the other landless Batwa. We want to give them what they need.

Aware of the challenges of land purchase for the Batwa, we make inquiry after inquiry but are rebuffed. After much pleading, George, the father of one of our employees, says he's willing to sell a piece of his land. George seems to understand the plight of the Batwa. His six-acre property is nearby and has an excellent water source. There is a hill on the property that will make a fine site for homes. The lower portion is rich, productive bottomland. Through our calculations, we learn that each Batwa family requires two acres for survival, but can subsist on one acre, if the land is very fertile.

George, however, is willing to sell only half of his land. Negotiations start with some difficulty as George has a fixed figure that he adamantly sticks to of 8,800,000 Uganda shillings or $4,400.

George informs me, "$4,400 is the cost for me to build a fine, new home."

I tell George, "We don't have the money."

George pauses for a bit then asks, "Would you buy the entire portion of land for 8,800,000 shillings?"

We now have a shot at obtaining all land that Flora and her extended family will need. I'm reinvigorated. We agree on the price. While I'm not sure how I'll do it, I promise him that I'll raise the money as quickly as possible.

The next day, Eileen and Graham Hodgetts, missionaries from Pittsburgh, visit us before returning to the States. Graham and Eileen are a delightful couple. Graham is an inventor, having designed a much-used helicopter flight simulator. Eileen is a best-selling author and a stage director, having won several Tony Awards. They have had three successful weeks working in Houma, a city two days' drive to the north of the Bwindi. They have established a coffee plantation and a U.S. distribution system for the beans. All the proceeds are returned to benefit development in the Houma area.

Graham's special interest is clean water. Using his design skills, he has developed a simple piece of equipment for digging wells. Eileen seems at home in any environment.

Eileen and Graham Hodgetts with a Batwa family

Graham and Eileen tell us that they need to safeguard a case containing some money remaining from their work in Houma. We lock their bag in a metal trunk in our bedroom. The following day, we hike up a steep slope that opens into a fertile valley where the Batwa village of Mukongoro is located. We arrive breathless but with enough residual energy to share in a joyful dance with the Batwa. Graham finds a good spot to dig a well. More dancing ensues.

Returning home, after dinner we sit on our porch enjoying the cool of the evening. Graham and Eileen inquire about the health status of the Batwa. They particularly want to know about Flora, whom they had met earlier in the day.

Carol explains, "For Batwa, like Flora and her family, land ownership is crucial for survival."

Eileen asks, "What are you going to do to help?"

I answer, "A local villager has in fact just offered his land for sale, but a donor hasn't been located."

"How much is the land?" they inquire.

"$4,400," I say.

A surprised look comes over their faces. Eileen says, "Do you realize that the amount we locked in your trunk is exactly $4,400? Please use it for Flora and her family!"

Carol and I grab Eileen and Graham and we dance about the room. Our prayers have been answered. When we settle down, we tell Eileen and Graham that their gift is much more than land. It is tangible evidence that God is in control and that He cares about the Batwa.

After Graham and Eileen depart, the land is purchased and Flora and six Batwa families move onto the property. We assist with the purchase of a few hoes and bags of seeds. The Batwa construct their own houses, dig pit latrines, and begin tilling the land. Flora and the families, who have lost many children to malnutrition, are now headed toward self-sufficiency and a brighter future.

Not too many years ago, the Batwa called the Bwindi rainforest their home. Their forcible removal from the forest was a grave injustice done to them by the Ugandan government—fueled, one might add, by the demand from tourists from rich nations eager to catch a glimpse of the exotic mountain gorilla. This sad history cannot be reversed. The great tragedy now is that the Batwa have no home at all. With land, they can find a new way to have a home, a stable abode where they can live together, raise crops, care for their young ones, raise them within a family and tribal history, and welcome visitors.

Months later, Carol and I are packing for a trip back to the States. We'll visit friends and family and, with luck, raise funds to build the medical clinic on the land we have recently acquired through the negotiating skill of Chief Elphaz. We hear a persistent knocking at the door. It is Flora. "Please come to my home quickly; my daughter Hope is in labor!"

I grab Nate, a Tulane Medical student, and run with Flora to assist Hope. Hope is in active labor. Nate cautions her against bearing down until the infant's head has descended further. Nevertheless, as soon as he turns his back, she places her feet against the wall and strains with all her might in an attempt to deliver the child. Fortunately, labor is not disrupted and eventually the time comes when she can be instructed to push.

A chorus of encouragement comes from her mother, relatives, and other friends in attendance. Although some of this encouragement consists of helpful advice, it is punctuated with yelps, cries, and rip-roaring laughter. It seems as if everyone is having a merry time, except Hope. At last, she gives a mighty push and Nate is cradling a newborn baby girl. When they hear the infant's cry, the Batwa break into full-throated songs of joy as Nate gently lays the infant on Hope's breast.

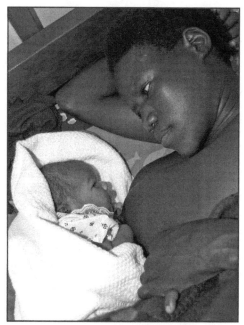

Hope and her first child

We return home under a canopy of stars. I direct Nate's attention to alpha and beta Centauri, which point toward the Southern Cross. For centuries, seamen have used the Southern Cross to navigate when sailing the southern hemisphere.

"We're under a different sky," Nate says, "but the joy of new life is the same the world over."

CHAPTER 18

✥ ✥ ✥

Discovering Abundance
in Community

"A tree cannot stand without roots."

━━ • Congolese Proverb • ━━

When we arrive in the U.S., we work to raise money for the construction of the clinic. We obtain promises of around $25,000, the bulk coming from one large church. At the end of our time, Carol and I visit Texas to say goodbye to her family. Our bags are packed. As usual, our luggage is crammed, and my carry-on is barely portable. Bathroom scales indicate that our bags have reached the maximum weight allowed for airline travel.

The day of departure, at a fund-raising gathering in the auditorium of a Houston church, I meet a dapper, well-dressed young man from Uganda. He is thrilled that we are returning to his home country. He has been in the U.S. for several months and misses his family in Kampala.

As I pour him a cup of coffee, he mentions, "My brother is considering starting a business that we believe will be successful. Would you be willing to carry over an item for him?"

Carol whispers that we might be able to squeeze in a small package, a book maybe.

I ask, "How can we help?"

He pauses for a while, "There are many dignitaries living in Kampala and my brother has noticed that they have manicured lawns. My brother is thinking about a lawn care business. Would you mind carrying over a lawnmower? I would like to purchase a nice riding one for him."

We barely hold back from laughing out loud. How much more can be expected of us? We still have so much to learn.

When we return to the Bwindi, we gather with the local people to discuss building the clinic. Well over five hundred villagers attend. I begin by thanking the elders and the landowners for the successful negotiations to acquire the land.

I then announce: "While in the U.S., we have raised sufficient funds to build a clinic."

The crowd is ecstatic; they jump to their feet, clapping, singing, and, as usual, dancing.

I yell over the din, "It will be difficult. It's more than just constructing a building. The clinic requires a staff of medical folks and those who will run the hospital."

More applause.

I continue, "It is important for us to work together. This clinic cannot be a *muzungu's* clinic. It should be owned and operated by you."

The villagers welcome this concept with frenzied delight.

Over the cacophony, I shout, "For this to happen, the community needs to pull together. All members need to cooperate; Christians, Muslims, Abafumu, Bakiga, Batwa, park employees, and the military."

All the energy in the room suddenly evaporates. A gloomy silence prevails.

A muted response comes from an elder, "We don't have anything in common. How can we possibly work together?"

Not having to yell anymore, I quietly tell them, "What we have in common is building a clinic that will prevent and treat the diseases in this area. We all have something we can learn from each other. We can inspire one another and grow together."

"But we have never worked together, how can we do this?" they lament.

I find myself surprised by their lack of willingness to cooperate. Searching for some solution, I tell them, "You need to form a committee of members from all the groups. I am willing to help."

The meeting ends with everyone dispirited. The villagers quietly drift away, heads bowed.

Carol acknowledges, "They have a lot to learn about collaboration, and so do we!"

It takes seven long months and innumerable meetings, but by the end of 2003 we form a committee that is willing to listen to each other and is committed to work together. I inform the U.S. donors that we are finally ready to build. I am devastated when they inform me that problems have arisen in their church, and they have used the money for other purposes.

I ask for another meeting of the villagers. The message is spread by word of mouth, and vigorous drumming announces the imminent gathering. A large crowd again attends.

I thank them for all the work that they have put into establishing the committee, but I reluctantly inform them, "There is no money for construction. It's all gone."

I gird myself for an onslaught of criticism, but instead of an outcry, there is just quiet acceptance. They sit in silence.

Chief Elphaz whispers to me, "Many projects fail; we expect the same with yours." Then he asks me, "Is there any money left in the building fund?"

I explain to him, "We have only $7,000 remaining, not the $25,000 we need to build the clinic."

"$7,000! That is a lot of money," he rejoins.

"But Chief, $7,000 is not even close to the amount needed to construct a clinic."

As I look for an opportunity to quietly escape, Chief Elphaz rises and informs the meeting, "Dr. Scort has $7,000 remaining for the clinic."

There is a buzz of excitement.

As I sit dejected, an elderly fellow stands and emphatically states, "With $7,000, we can purchase roofing material and concrete."

Another adds, "My village will build the foundation."

One after the other, different local leaders chime in:

"My clan can carry stones."

"My clan can provide the labor."

"We have a truck."

The committee quickly convenes and agrees that $7,000 is adequate and announces, "Construction will begin immediately."

Several days later, the elders assemble at first light, each holding a unique horn. At an appointed time, each elder, in turn, stands and blows a clear distinct note that initiates a series of drumbeats in the distance. This is the call for members of each clan to assemble to begin their labors. People stream in from far and wide. They dig the foundation, carry stones, and erect walls. With everyone working together, a wonderful structure—our new clinic—is completed in under two months, and the $7,000 has not been exhausted!

We use the remaining money to throw the customary dedication ceremony. It is a great feast; cows, goats, and chickens are prepared, a mountain of bananas is cooked, and the local brew flows in abundance. Over one thousand people from the surrounding villages join the celebration. Animated dance routines are performed, and we celebrate together with great exuberance. A clinic is born.

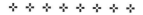

In the wee hours of the morning, as the music winds down and villagers depart, Elphaz and I talk about how wonderful the celebration has been. Elphaz says in a hushed voice, "The real joy will be that our children survive. We won't hear the constant wailing of mothers."

Months later, I overhear a conversation between a local elder and a patient who has arrived from a distant village. This patient is commenting on the quality of the construction, noting, "It is nice that a rich *muzungu* builds such a fine clinic for you."

The elder is incensed, and says to the patient, "A *muzungu* helps, but this community builds this clinic. It is not a *muzungu* clinic, it is the community's clinic!"

He marches the visitor over to the entrance. "Look what this sign says: BWINDI COMMUNITY HEALTH CENTRE. This is a community clinic. We own it and we operate it."

The loss of funds promised from America that I had considered so devastating instead results in an enormous blessing and a gift.

The beginning of the Bwindi Community Health Center

CHAPTER 19

✦ ✦ ✦

Out of Stock

"Coffee and love taste best when hot."

━━ • Ethiopian Proverb • ━━

Obtaining adequate medical supplies for the clinic is a huge struggle. While most of our supplies are purchased at cost at the Joint
Medical Store, operated by the Anglican and Catholic Churches,
we are dependent on the Ugandan government to provide essential
drugs not available elsewhere, especially for the treatment of tuberculosis, HIV/AIDS, and leprosy. These medications are sent from the
Ugandan government to the District Medical Office where they are
distributed to clinics.

On an excursion to the District Medical Office, I attempt to replen-
ish our stock of depleted medications while Carol visits friends who
live nearby. In the U.S., government offices can drive a person a bit
crazy; Ugandan government offices have the power to permanently
institutionalize! With a low threshold for bureaucratic pain, I can
quickly become a person I don't recognize.

I can only hope that, after a two-hour drive, the District Medical
Officer is available. I enter a rambling, poorly lit building, with a
maze of hallways branching toward darkened offices that appear as
if they have not been occupied for quite some time. It's a relief to
see a dim light escaping underneath the door of the District Medical
Officer's secretary. I enter and meet a woman with artfully plaited

hair, intently concentrating on her computer screen. She greets me with a consuming silence.

After a while, I clear my throat to remind her of my presence. Her response is still silence.

Finally, I inquire, "Is the District Medical Officer in?"

Without a word, eyes still glued to her screen, she points towards an adjacent door. I carefully follow the arc of her finger to make sure that I locate the correct door. As I pass, I peer at her screen and offer, "If you move the seven of hearts under the eight of clubs, then you can free up that face-down card. If you are lucky, it will be the ace that you need!"

She doesn't seem to appreciate my advice. My sarcasm, however, noticeably lifts my own spirits. Maintenance of an even disposition is mandatory when visiting these officials.

The District Medical Officer is a supplicant's worst nightmare. He's a short, reedy fellow with bullet eyes, dressed in a well-pressed suit several sizes too large. He sits in a cavernous room, behind a desk piled high with documents whose urgency, given the layers of dust, expired long ago. Chairs splay out from the desk in the otherwise barren room.

He motions me to sit nearby. Peering around a stack of papers, he asks, "How may I help?"

I pull out my list. "Our clinic has run out of tuberculosis medications."

Before I can continue, he waves me to silence and intones, "Out of stock."

"But if tuberculosis medications are discontinued in mid-therapy, drug resistance can develop," I plead.

"Out of stock."

Trying to sound more positive, he says, "I'd like to help you, but my hands are tied."

"Perhaps you have birth control pills?"

"Out of stock."

"How about some condoms?" I persist.

He now shows some animation. "We recently received several crates of the Engabu condoms. They are supported by the Government of Uganda."

I pause, "But I thought that Engabu condoms were recalled because they are defective."

The medical officer counters with a knowing grin, "I have been informed that they work most of the time!"

"That's just great. How about HIV test kits?"

"We expect them any day; but, out of stock."

"It seems test kits have been unavailable for quite some time."

"Yes, it's been eighteen months since we had HIV testing materials, but they could arrive at any moment."

I depart with several thousand defective condoms, hoping, along with the medical officer, that they will work "most of the time."

Roadside medicine

When I pick up Carol, she enquires, "Did you find any empathy in there?"

"Out of stock," I reply.

Returning to the Bwindi, we pass a thin, young fellow lying on a mat in a fetal position, surrounded by several women. His mother sits next to him swishing away flies. It is not uncommon to find patients lingering by the roadway, afflicted with severe malaria, semi-comatose, and close to death. The family sits, patiently waiting for someone to pass, trusting that the unfortunate victim can be transported to the nearest medical facility several hours away. I am amazed by their faith, as there are no buses or taxis on these roads.

Although we are driving a well-marked ambulance, there is no joyous waving, and we are not even motioned to stop. The family just sits in quiet desperation, ready to accept the inevitable.

We jump out of the ambulance, greet the family, and ask about the boy. The story is all too familiar. He was healthy until recently but is now afflicted by a high fever and is unable to walk or speak. It's obviously malaria. I start an IV, infuse glucose, and give a loading dose of quinine. As usual, my roadside ministrations attract a crowd of onlookers.

We load the patient into our vehicle and several family members pile in, requesting that we transport him to a small medical clinic near their village. As the family is penniless, we deposit them at the clinic with the medicine necessary for the course of the illness and a small sum to pay for nursing care and food.

"*Webare munonga*" the words for "thank you," are rarely exchanged. As everyone contributes to the benefit of the community, it is assumed that what you do to assist will eventually be repaid.

Ten days later, as I work at a mobile outreach, a boy approaches me with his hand extended and sporting a wide gleaming grin. I am surprised when he says, "*Webare Munonga, nojuna amagara gangye,*" (Thank you, you save my life).

I ask him how we met. He continues, "My family carries me to the roadside where you find me. You stop, stick a needle in my arm, and you take my family and me to the clinic. I walk here to thank you. We're poor; I can't repay the shillings you give my family. I'm in school; I will be a doctor and help folks along the road. I owe you my life."

Over dinner that night, I confide to Carol, "I am overjoyed about what that boy told me today, but I'm torn about how I should be using my time to reach the most people. The price of caring is high, not only in money for building clinics and acquiring supplies, but also in time and effort. I'm worried that I am not finding enough time for us."

Carol is well aware that the innumerable nights when I have been awakened to attend to a medical emergency are taking their toll. The required constant availability to patients has been hard on both of us. She sighs, "All we can do is our best as we see it. I feel that we are giving as much as we are able. I feel sure that's all God asks of us."

CHAPTER 20

✢ ✢ ✢

A Thin Veil Between
the Living and the Dead

"When an old man dies, a library burns to the ground."

———— • West African Proverb • ————

Security is a concern at the Bwindi, especially around our new clinic. On March 1, 1999, the world awoke to horrific news from the Bwindi. A force of 100 to 150 former Rwandan Interahamwe guerrillas, the perpetrators of the Rwandan genocide in 1994, infiltrated the Bwindi Impenetrable Park from the DRC. They kidnapped fourteen foreign tourists and their Ugandan guide. While they eventually released six, they murdered the remaining eight. Records indicate that two of the victims were found with handwritten notes attached to their bodies that read: "This is the punishment for the Anglo-Saxons who sold us. You protect the minority and oppress the majority."

News of the deaths spread quickly. The incident is well documented by Mark Ross, a safari guide, in his book *Dangerous Beauty*. Mark was one of those abducted, along with his clients. The incident left the tourism industry, especially gorilla trekking, in serious jeopardy. Ever since, there has been a military presence at the Bwindi. Tourists who trek the mountain gorillas are accompanied by rangers armed with AK-47s. Military patrols travel at night along the border of the DRC, attempting to prevent any further incursions.

Three years after this incident, Carol and I attended a memorial for the victims of the massacre. It is a sedate affair presided over by the British High Commissioner, who dedicates a plaque to the deceased. The names of the American dead are missing; it could be that the American families did not want any remembrances of their demise. At dinner, we sit across from an attractive, well-dressed African woman. She tosses her long braids aside as she reigns in her lively three-year-old.

I ask her, "How did you happen to come to such an event?"

Her smile disappeared. "My husband was the ranger who was tortured. I was pregnant at the time with this child. He never saw his daughter. It was difficult then, but it is better now. I still don't understand how one person can brutalize another. Our daughter reminds me of him. I miss him very much, but my life goes on."

At the Bwindi Community Health Center (BCHC), Ugandan military personnel guard the facility at night and we receive regular security updates regarding potential rebel movements. At one meeting with the military, the Bwindi Park warden, and other security personnel, I express my dismay, "Why have you withdrawn the military team that has been protecting our clinic? Are the rebels no longer a problem?"

They shrug, offering no explanation, so I continue. "The BCHC pharmacy has drugs, and we have an accounting department where money is stored. In addition, we train medical students from around the world, who live on site. Rebels from the DRC attacked a small health unit nearby six months ago. Four weeks ago, an armed man killed one person and wounded three others before being slain only a few yards from where we sit. Three days ago, rebels killed a local citizen, and recently, several thousand refugees, escaping the war in the DRC, fled to a refugee camp nearby. Doesn't security at the BCHC seem like an issue that needs addressing?"

The security personnel agree, "The BCHC is a potential target. Any murdered or tortured *bazungu* will reflect poorly on the Ugandan government and on us. It would adversely affect tourism."

Carol whispers to me, "Most tourists would not choose to include torture as part of their all-inclusive vacation package!"

The head of the military announces, "Perhaps a squad of five military personnel stationed at the BCHC, a machine gun nest, and at least one rocket launcher. That should repel an attack."

The proposal pleases everyone.

The Bwindi Warden suggests, "We need to celebrate the successful conclusion of our discussions. Why don't we move to one of the tourist camps for a cup of tea?"

As we pour out the door, I offer: "I'll pay."

When we arrive at the lodge, a round of beer is poured.

So much for teatime!

After the first round, Carol and I are tired and ready to return home. However, the park warden proposes, "Just one more round to toast the success of the meeting."

They all congratulate me on my input. Most of all, they appreciate my acceptance of the tab. After the fourth round of beer, the conversation becomes very animated. Several people give spirited, unintelligible speeches, and many go for additional rounds. Finally, awash in friendship and beer, everyone retires to their quarters. A job well done!

As we walk home, Carol wonders if anything we discussed will be remembered in the morning.

Several months later, on a bright September day, four Ugandan military vehicles, bristling with machine guns and rocket launchers, screech to a halt in front of BCHC. An officer dressed in combat fatigues and shiny boots, with a revolver at his hip, approaches me, announcing, "There has been a rebel attack on a village; please come with me!" It is apparent that "no" is not an acceptable answer.

The troops rush me on a forty-five-minute, bone-jarring ride. We stop suddenly and exit the military vehicles and begin rapidly ascending a steep slope toward a small village on the border of the DRC. The unrelenting African sun beats down on me and the air is dank following a recent rainstorm. Wearing a white lab coat, perspiring profusely, and panting for air, I'm in stark contrast to the twenty-five Ugandan soldiers surrounding me. Despite wearing heavy, green fatigues and carrying AK-47s and rocket launchers, the soldiers don't break a sweat as they jog up the path.

I pray that the villagers have been able to escape the wrath of the rebels, but as we approach, a horrible sight unfolds. A lone figure lies in a contorted position with several deep cuts across his back and a single bullet hole at the base of his skull. His clothes are rags, and he was obviously unarmed. What sort of person would kill the defenseless?

Our progress along the trail reveals more death and destruction: bodies lie like rag dolls carelessly tossed aside, landing in unnatural positions. Smoke curls from the simple grass huts that have been set on fire. Friends and relatives of the dead are milling about, sifting through the carnage. I see their expressionless faces. The sun slides behind a few clouds, casting an eerie light on the scene.

My medical skills are useless. There are no survivors. The same shot to the back of the head and machete marks are gruesomely replicated one helpless victim after the next.

The hair on my neck bristles when a woman nearby releases a piercing scream, "This is my husband!"

I kneel to comfort her as best I can, but what can I say?

I am used to people dying. In my more than thirty years of practicing medicine in the U.S., most of the deaths I have observed have occurred in controlled hospital environments or at a patient's home assisted by hospice care. In these circumstances, expressions of comfort come easily. "He lived a good life," or "At least she didn't have to suffer."

On this bloody hillside, such words are hollow. I feel helpless and angry. There are no courses in medical school on ministering to a plundered village. I can't begin to imagine the personal agony of sifting through the bodies hunting for a family member. There is the lingering smell of gunpowder; but there is another persistent, noxious aroma: the stench of evil.

My thoughts are interrupted when a villager asks, "Please, come with me."

The military allows me to accompany the villager, but cautions, "The rebels have probably disappeared and melted back across the border, but stragglers may still be around."

The villagers include me as they make a large circle around the victims. They begin singing softly. As the song progresses, their voices lift, and they sway together. The song gathers momentum as tears flow.

I ask the man holding my hand, "What are the words that are being sung?"

He relates, "It is an ancient song of healing. *Nagasan*, our God, must bring comfort to the community; without this healing, there will be more death."

The singing continues, much more spirited as the tempo increases.

"What about this song?" I inquire.

"It's a prayer asking *Nagasan* to forgive the offenders. Without forgiveness, the community will never truly be restored and healed."

I'm pierced to the heart.

The singing continues, but a military official taps me on the shoulder, barking at me, "It is not safe for you to stay; we have to leave—NOW!"

As I make my way down the mountain, accompanied by the heavily armed military, the singing fades into the background. The curtain of desperation and despair begins to lift. The villagers' prayers reveal a deep sense of God's presence in such suffering. There is hope for healing.

✤ ✤ ✤ ✤ ✤ ✤ ✤ ✤

It is apparent that here in sub-Saharan Africa there is only the hint of a division between sorrow and joy, death and life.

I see this again in a different way when I am asked to attend the funeral of an elderly Mutwa named Kafumbiri. Kafumbiri lived at a remote Batwa settlement and had recently succumbed to an acute illness. When I arrive, Batwa from many settlements have gathered to remember him, supporting his family and singing their traditional songs of grief. Dancing, drinking, and happiness abound, effortlessly combining with the more somber elements of the ceremony. Nearby, several Batwa are busily pounding nails into a rough, planked coffin.

I sit with the relatives as they lament Kafumbiri's death. It is obvious that he will be sorely missed. I ask them to tell me about him:

"A fine man, always happy."

"He never misses a party."

"He spends all he has on local brew, but he always shares."

"He does not work, but he can sing and dance!"

"We love Kafumbiri."

It seems that Kafumbiri had a sobriety issue but was the life of the party and well loved.

They ask, "Do you want to see him before we place him in the coffin?"

"Sure, I would be honored to say goodbye."

They escort me to a shabby mud hut. I enter a darkened room where the small, shriveled frame of Kafumbiri lies still on a mat. He seems at peace in his final repose, a beatific smile on thin lips, spindly arms folded over his chest, small, wrinkled hands protruding from a threadbare coat.

I quietly sit next to the body and whisper a prayer, "God, please bless this man. He was well loved and enjoyed his time on earth."

A fly alights on his face and, as I reach over to flip it off, I notice that his face is still warm. I run my hand down his neck and detect a faint carotid pulse. Although severely dehydrated and comatose, Kafumbiri is pre-moribund; but he's not dead!

I quickly exit the hut and announce to the crowd: "*Kafumbiri taine yafa!* Kafumbiri lives!"

All activity ceases. They silently stare at me with a look of great surprise. Suddenly, a loud cheer erupts (although some seem a bit irked by this turn of events, especially the coffin makers).

We load Kafumbiri into my vehicle for transport to the hospital. As we depart, the revelry picks up in intensity, with the new hope that Kafumbiri will return to share in more good times.

I evaluate Kafumbiri at the BCHC and find that he is in septic shock. We pump in intravenous fluids and antibiotics. He recovers. With a combination of no alcohol and fine hospital food, mentally and physically he returns to normal and even puts on a few pounds.

A joyful Kafumbiri

A few weeks later, as I drive him back to his village, I wonder what the response will be. Kafumbiri seems amused when I quote him a proverb, "*Yeshushanirize nkomufu, oboone kumanya noha arakukunda,*" (Pretend that you are dead, and you will find out who truly loves you). On arrival he is greeted warmly, the Batwa stream out their huts with much singing and dancing. Kafumbiri scowls at the partially finished coffin lying nearby.

Thereafter, every time I meet Kafumbiri, he flashes his characteristic toothless grin, lighting up his face. He grasps me by both arms and exclaims, "I am so happy to be above the ground! Please join me for a brew!"

CHAPTER 21

✣ ✣ ✣

Visionary Friends

"What an old man sees while sitting,
a young man cannot see standing."

—— • West African Proverb • ——

In its first two years of operation, the Bwindi Community Health Center becomes a major success, yet Carol and I often discuss the difficult path toward its sustainability. As we have noticed, it is common in Africa for a project to begin with a bang, only later to disappear with hardly a trace. We realize that we need an organization to provide us with oversight and wise guidance. Just then, Dick Panzica appears on our radar. Dick is an instructor in celestial navigation for U-2 pilots at California's Beale Air Force Base. Dick's ramrod straight posture and focused demeanor indicate a close attachment to the military. His bald head, close cropped mustache, generous smile, and love of the U-2 program have earned him the nickname "U-2 Godfather." Dick had heard me speak at his church and was persuaded that he needed to assist. He invited a group of his U-2 pilot friends to his house and convinced them of the need to form a 501(c)(3) foundation to support us. Around Dick's kitchen table, the Kellermann Foundation is born. This foundation becomes our oversight and our guide. Sure, we know more about running a health center than they do, but they know a lot more about sustaining an organization. It's a symbiotic and fruitful relationship.

Dick teams up with a consummate Rotarian, Don Fultz. Don focuses not on the money, but rather on making a difference; his ability to fundraise is exceptional. Don's good humor, warm handshake, and sunny demeanor are irresistible to donors. Don gives me a copy of his humorous memoirs regarding his forays into real-estate called *How I Lost $1,000,000 in Real Estate - Using Nothing Down*. Don and Dick lift us up when we fall, offer endless encouragement, and supply vision and focus on how best to assist the Batwa.

Dick and Don eventually turn the Foundation's board chairmanship over to Dr. Simi Lyss and the executive directorship to Sally Stillings. Operating stateside, these two are an incredible team. Although Sally's training is in physical therapy, she has expanded her skills into in organizational development. Sally has a heart for those less fortunate and an intense spiritual motivation blended with a generous nature. Simi is quite eclectic; he is a dermatologist, engineer, graphic designer, and a former medical administrator with Kaiser Permanente. His people skills are exceptional. I nickname Simi the "Seven-Eleven Dude" because he is a one stop shop for information regarding running a hospital. Sally and Simi are aware of the potential of BCHC. Currently, BCHC is primarily an outpatient facility; there is no access to blood transfusions or other medical or surgical care. Children requiring transfusions, mothers who need advanced maternity care, and individuals needing complex treatment must be transferred to a distant government hospital. Sally and Simi are visionaries; they encourage the construction of a top-tier, in-patient hospital for the Batwa and many others living in the region.

While I am in the U.S., I give Simi the Uganda Ministry of Health's plans for clinics and hospitals. The diagrams have obvious design flaws, and the designed structures are not visually appealing. They seem quite dark and inhospitable. Simi carefully studies the government templates, pulls out a legal pad, straight edge, and sharpened pencils, and gets to work. He appropriates the general measurements that the government specifies but makes adjustments to allow for easily accessible rooms that flow well. He designed the hospital to be centered around a large courtyard. Simi intuitively understands the cultural necessity of providing gathering places and fostering community. Taking advantage of ambient light, he incorporates large windows and translucent skylights into his design. He then adds the final ingredient: personality. The hospital will be both warm and welcoming.

Simi's drawings require Ugandan government approval. When I return to Uganda, I steel my nerves for trouble. True to expectations, when I hand the plans to the local district engineer, he glances them over and quickly tosses them back. "How can I possibly sanction such a radical departure from the government design?" My spirits are crushed when he adds, "You must go to Kampala to obtain permission from the Ministry of Health."

Following a grueling overnight bus ride, I arrive at the Ministry of Health. The folks who occupy these offices are chosen because they are either successful at their jobs or relatives of those in power. I hope for the former. I am directed to a web of offices that have no obvious signage. It's worse than I expected. I'm bounced from one office to another with the repetitive mantra, "We have no authority. Perhaps someone down the hall can help." Each room that I enter is filled with expectant patrons who seem to have been waiting for hours. I pray that I will escape the building with my sanity intact. At the very end of the day, I am finally directed to the Ministry of Health's Engineering Department.

I ask to see the chief engineer. However, the secretary tells me, "It is late, and as this is Friday, he probably has gone home for the weekend. Perhaps you can come back Monday."

If this is the first step in building a hospital, I wonder how any institutions of healing are ever constructed. My journey appears utterly futile; however, as I am slowly rolling up the drawings, an engineer walks by.

"What do we have here?" he inquires, taking the plans from me.

"Oh, these are designs for a new hospital at the Bwindi."

He looks over the plans and comments, "There are no hospitals in that area. The government would welcome one. Wow, I see you have skylights. The patient flow patterns are good, and the space is well utilized. Please wait here."

I breathe a sigh of relief in finding a well-educated and caring engineer.

Walking down the hall, he knocks on doors, telling other engineers, "Come and see these hospital drawings!"

Soon, engineers surround the plans. One engineer comments on the quantity of windows, another on the skylights. Others note that the hallways are minimal, freeing up space for patient care, and that patients are visible from the nurses' station.

While I agree with the engineers' assessments of the plans, they still require approval. I inquire if the chief engineer is present.

The first engineer I met raises his hand. Yes!

Rummaging in his suitcase, he produces a government stamp and quickly signs the documents. Then, he asks if he can copy the plans for his file to use as a reference for future government hospitals. Almost delirious with relief, I hand the plans over. As he heads for the copy machine, my thoughts are swirling.

I return to the Bwindi on the night bus, mission accomplished.

Carol is thrilled with my results, too. But she tempers my joy, remarking, "Now all we have to do is figure out how to pay for it."

CHÅPTER 22

✤ ✤ ✤

Lessons in Generosity

"Giving is not losing, it is keeping for tomorrow."

──── • Zambia Proverb • ────

Raising money from a distant and remote area is always a challenge. A long trip to Kampala to an internet café is required to send out our large file newsletters. We combine these trips with visiting friends who work for non-governmental or aid organizations. They tell us about the many parties held in Kampala where they meet and greet potential donors. These fundraising parties sound like fun, especially the tasty food, but the fourteen-to-sixteen-hour bus ride hinders our attendance.

We don't have any regular donor support, and every month, we are scrambling to make ends meet. Lately, we've been going through an especially difficult stretch. We are barely able to pay our clinic staff, so any construction is out of the question. Carol's mother has been generous, as have a few friends, but most of our donations are in the range of $5 to $500. We've also tapped into our savings and sold some of our property in California to meet obligations. Not only are our resources nearly depleted, so is our hope. Posted on the clinic's wall are Simi's well-delineated hospital plans. The drawings seem like a mirage—a great idea going nowhere. Carol and I hold hands and pray for a financial godsend.

A week later, I am driving five Batwa women, each cradling a severely ill child, to a government hospital for medical care. These kids are anemic and require life-saving blood transfusions. As I pass a grass landing strip, where wealthy tourists arrive for gorilla trekking, I stop to watch a familiar plane bank over the hills. It cuts power and bounces along the uneven airstrip. The craft comes to a halt near my ambulance and the pilot exits, sporting a huge smile. I have known John for several years. He is a consummate bush pilot and looks the part: tanned, dapper, and sporting an aviator hat, the sides of which are molded downward from decades of wearing headphones.

I ask jokingly, "Did you receive any ground-fire?"

This airstrip is adjacent to the DRC; while taking off and landing, planes violate Congolese airspace. Occasionally, the pilot, and especially the passengers, are startled by fire from AK-47 wielding, trigger-happy Congolese rebels.

He laughs, "No flak, only outstanding views."

John notices my anxiousness and asks what's going on. I unload: "I have sick children in the ambulance who desperately need transfusions. It's likely the government hospital we're headed to will not have blood, which means driving to the more distant mission hospital. It's their only chance for survival."

With John's "Good luck, you and the kids will need it!" ringing in my ears, I head off to the hospital.

My fears are realized. There's no blood at the government hospital. We drive on to the mission hospital and are well received by the nurses. I return from the eight-hour round trip exhausted but hopeful that the children will survive. I later learn that one didn't make it.

Three days later, a van appears at our clinic carrying guests from an upscale lodge. These guests, I learn, were the passengers on John's recent flight. One of them, Howard Blair, leans out the window and requests, "Can you take me on a quick tour of the clinic?"

I tell him, "Let's go! Our clinic is small, only a few examination rooms and an area for deliveries. In a matter of minutes, you will have seen everything."

Howard exits the van, greeting me with a wide smile and a vigorous handshake. He seems to have something on his mind. During our quick swing through the clinic, Howard asks a few questions, mainly concerning the needs of the area and our plans for expansion.

When we return to the van, he asks, "How can I make out the check?"

"A check?" I wonder. We have never received a check.

I tell Howard to please make it out to the Bwindi Community Health Center. He scribbles on the check, hands it to me, and enters the van.

I open the check expecting at most $500—and indeed, the first number is a five, but there are more and more zeroes. The zeros add up to a breathtaking $50,000! I can't believe what I am seeing.

I race to the departing van and pound on the side for it to stop.

When it slows, Howard's head appears out the window. I thank him for the donation, then ask, "Why are you so generous?"

He says, "I'll write soon and tell you the story."

Several weeks later, I receive this email from Howard: "Many years ago, I felt asked by God to contribute to a charity, but I put it off. I was plagued by insomnia and finally became convinced that I wouldn't get a good night's sleep until I made a substantial contribution, which I did. On the recent flight to the Bwindi, my heart raced when the plane banked and was plummeting toward a postage-stamp-sized grass field. When we finally bounced to a stop, I quickly exited, giving thanks to John and to God that both the plane and I were in one piece. It was then that I overheard your conversation with John about the anemic children. I thought at the time that I might make a donation. This was confirmed when I did not sleep for several days. I have slept soundly ever since I handed you the check!"

Several weeks later, Jolie and Ian McTavish, having just trekked to visit the gorillas, arrive to see the clinic. Ian is uncomfortable visiting severely ill patients, so while I take Jolie on a tour of the hospital,

Ian and Carol stay at the guesthouse.

Relaxing over a cup of tea, after a bit of small talk, Ian asks Carol what the clinic needs. Surprised by this rarely asked question, Carol collects herself and tells him, "Rural Uganda has some of the highest maternal mortality rates on the planet. We need to be able to perform Cesarean

Jolie McTavish and friends

sections for pregnant women who can't deliver normally. We're trying to raise money for a surgical unit."

"How much would that cost?"

Carol smiles, "$50,000 should do the trick."

Undaunted, Ian asks, "Do you take checks?"

Carol's eyes widen, "Do we ever!"

As he makes out the check, Carol asks him what prompted this tremendous act of kindness.

Ian replies, "Of course I'm doing this to help save the pregnant mothers, but I am also doing it for my beloved mother, Joan Mary. Will you please name the operating theater after her? Joan Mary was an emergency room nurse and was truly dedicated to the profession of medicine."

Carol profusely thanks Ian, promising to remember Joan Mary and his generosity.

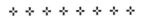

Another month passes and Carol and I are sipping a beverage at a local tourist lodge. Our clinic lacks refrigeration, so it is a rare treat to savor a cool drink.

Jon Holt, a good-looking, well-groomed, tanned fellow, dressed in safari gear, is seated at a nearby table talking with his wife Bev.

Jon leans over and asks, "Have you trekked the gorillas?"

"No. Carol and I live here; the gorillas come to see us."

Confused, Jon asks me, "What are you doing here?"

"I am a physician."

"You mean that there's a hospital here?" Jon exclaims.

"Well, sort of."

Jon persists, "Tell me about your work and what you're trying to accomplish."

"My specialty is tropical diseases. Although there are plenty of infectious diseases that keep me busy, our clinic is primarily focused on maternal and child health."

"What are your major challenges?"

"That's easy Jon," I respond. "There are too many preventable deaths of children under age five."

"What is required to address these deaths?" he asks.

"A children's unit would be helpful."

"How much will a unit cost?"

"Oh, I think around $50,000 would do."

"Okay, I'll send the money as soon as I return to the States."

Carol and I look at one another speechless. When she finds her voice, Carol tells Jon and Bev, "There is a local expression: 'Children are the reward of life.' Your gift will bring many rewards."

After several years of receiving only small donations, the spontaneous generosity of a few strangers provides $150,000. Our prayers have been answered and we have the cash to prove it! Churchill's quote takes on a new meaning for us, "We make a living by what we get, we make a life by what we give."

We now have the finances to expand our small outpatient clinic to an inpatient facility following Simi's design. Construction proceeds briskly. A temporary cloud descends when the district engineer arrives for an inspection, clipboard in hand. Noticing the skylights, he immediately says, "The skylights must be covered; they deviate from the Government's plans."

I direct the district engineer's attention to the Ugandan Ministry of Health's written permission and add, "If there is a problem, you may contact the chief engineer at the Ministry of Health in Kampala."

He departs, grumbling.

We are allowed to proceed with the construction. In a few years, the government of Uganda will issue revised guidelines for the construction of a clinic/hospital incorporating many of Simi's designs, skylights included. Borrowing again from Churchill, "We shape our buildings and thereafter they shape us." The hospital will be shaped by love, respect, and kindness.

Hospital expansion in Uganda involves far fewer headaches than in the United States. As a result, the newly renamed Bwindi Community Hospital (BCH) grows rather quickly from thirty-five to fifty beds. For comparison, a medium sized rural hospital in the U.S. has a capacity of twenty-five to forty-four beds.

In addition to hiring staff, Carol and I are supervising and managing the hospital. We have assembled a basic management team that includes several of the village elders. Their resumes do not include prior management experience, but they do have tremendous enthusiasm. We are like a family. Our meetings are typically fun-filled affairs over a meal or tea. While comradery abounds, the group has some difficulty actually getting down to business.

BCH's management committee agrees that meeting the hospital's operating expenses is a challenge. BCH cannot depend on patient fees for its main revenue; the majority of our patients have incomes under one dollar per day. Ninety-four percent of our costs must be supported by donations from the U.S.

The economics of running a hospital are daunting; even more so are the demands of administration, accounting, logistics, and human resources. It quickly becomes a heavy load. After dinner one night, Carol and I sit together on the porch listening to a forest alive with sound. Our discussions have lately focused on how direct contact with the Batwa has disappeared. We remember the joys of the days of mobile clinics. Carol laments, "While I am proud that BCH is improving the health of the Batwa, I cannot enjoy the results. I'm stuck in an office doing accounting."

I attempt to make light of her predicament by asking, "Besides accounting, you must love the logistics side, like getting the supplies from Kampala?"

From the look that I receive, it's obvious my joke is not well received.

I confess, "I love the practice of medicine. It's a big reason why I get out of bed in the morning. But medical practice has been replaced with interminable management meetings, personnel squabbles, and dealing with hospital funding gaps."

Carol nods and says "We've become victims of our own success. I fear that if we continue, we'll lose heart. Important things will fall between the cracks. We have to find a solution that allows the hospital to function smoothly and permits our lives to return to normal."

Help comes in the form of Rotary International, and, particularly, Jerry Hall. Jerry is a former international vice president of Rotary International and has Rotarian friends the world over. Tall and warmhearted with a commanding presence, the locals aptly name him "*Muzungu Silverback*," as Jerry's white hair reminds them of the white-striped, dominant, silverback leader of a gorilla troop. He has come to the Bwindi with a Rotary group for three weeks to assist with the installation of medical equipment due to arrive in a forty-foot container. However, delays in the overland transport of the container to the docks of San Francisco resulted in it missing the ship bound for Mombasa (the container actually arrives three months after the group departs). So, Jerry and his friends cannot do the very task they have traveled so far to undertake. The thought of Rotarians wandering around the Bwindi for three weeks with nothing to do is not appealing. Fortunately, Carol recalls Jerry's expertise in institutional organization and strategic planning, and she suggests these abilities are what we need, even more than medical supplies.

Tasha and Jerry Hall with Batwa

We explain our dilemma to Jerry, and he readily accepts the challenge. We gather our management team together. After tea, introductions, and greetings, Jerry passes out notebooks and pens.

The first question that Jerry asks is, "What do you see as the factors that would end our hospital project immediately?"

The management team members diligently write in their notebooks, compare answers, and become very animated. One of them offers, "We can come up with only two issues. Number one: If the rebels from nearby DRC come across the border and kill everyone."

Jerry remarks, "I've been asking this question to businesses for several decades and have never heard this answer before."

The team member continues, "Number two: We could not possibly continue if Carol and Scott were to leave."

Carol and I look at each other with dismay. We were not expecting this answer. Carol asks, "Are we in the same category as a rebel attack?"

Incredulous, I ask Jerry, "Am I to understand that we are indispensable?"

Carol reframes, "You mean that the hospital cannot exist without us?"

Jerry nods.

Carol and I slump in our chairs. I suggest yet another tea break where we can privately confer with Jerry.

We ask Jerry, "Are we required to stay for a lifetime?"

"We have not considered a succession plan."

"Is there a way out of this morass that will allow for the hospital to be sustainable and give us the freedom to come and go? We love the Batwa, and the hospital is surely helping them, but Carol and I realize that the effort of running it is getting in the way of building relationships with them."

Jerry simply states, "Your condition is not unusual; I have counseled other organizations in a similar state."

His next words deeply touch us: "You have given much to the Batwa and to this hospital. Perhaps, it's time for you to relinquish the responsibilities and to relax and enjoy your time at the Bwindi."

We look at each other and then back at Jerry, nodding, "That's what we want."

Jerry suggests to the management committee that an organizational structure must be put in place that will allow the hospital to manage and support itself without Carol's and my constant attention. We retool the management team and hire the necessary staff: an accountant, account assistants, logistics and procurement officers, human resource personnel, and administrators. Over the next year, twelve additional staff are employed. Some arrive with appropriate skills, others we train. Although our expenses increase, we operate much more smoothly and efficiently. This transition takes time to accomplish, but it results in Ugandans leading and managing the hospital.

The best outcome? Carol is smiling again.

CHAPTER 23

✤ ✤ ✤

Insurance Plans

"No one can use another's teeth to smile."

 • African Proverb • ———

We make arrangements for sharing administrative responsibilities and I am able to step down as superintendent of BCH. Dr. Paul Williams, on assignment from England with Volunteer Service Overseas, takes my place. Paul is the epitome of an Englishman. He has a clipped, precise, British accent, feels comfortable in his position of authority, is very proper in his attire, and is exceedingly intelligent.

I continue work as a doctor in the hospital and confer with Paul and others about crucial challenges for the long-term good of the hospital. A key challenge comes with the fact that as the hospital grows, the cost of health care also increases. A serious medical illness can be devastating financially for a patient, and while recuperating, they can't work. Our patients have become accustomed to being treated for a nominal charge, and if unable to pay, their debt is forgiven. We realize this policy will never allow for sustainability.

The situation becomes more acute when we open the surgical unit, which triggers a dramatic increase in our costs. Our charges are modest by American standards, but a seventy-dollar fee for a Cesarean section is overwhelming here in rural Uganda. When I discharge a patient on whom I've operated, I often overhear comments such as *"Tinyine sente, ninteekwa kuguza eitaka neinga embuzi,"* (I do not have money, I will have to sell land or my goats). It saddens me that while the patients leave the hospital healed, they descend further into poverty. The dilemma of how to deliver high-quality health care in a resource-poor setting remains daunting.

To address these issues, Paul has been talking with an NGO in Kampala regarding the possibility of a health-insurance scheme. They are considering a plan rather similar to the Western model where a premium is paid annually and care is rendered freely, excepting for a small co-pay at the time of service. Many are doubtful that such a proposal is tenable in this setting. Most villagers are unfamiliar with a future tense, so the concept of health insurance to cover a future event doesn't compute.

Our initial efforts into community-based health insurance are met with various obstacles. We have numerous discussions and "participatory development" meetings with the community. From a cost assessment of health care provision at BCH, we learn that we have been vastly undercharging for services. For example, our two-dollar charge for a delivery does not come close to covering the twelve-dollar expense. In order to encourage participation, we decide that those who do not register for insurance will be required to pay the increased hospital charges. As most villages have a radio, we launch a radio campaign marketing the new insurance plan, also announcing the increased hospital charges.

We feel satisfied by our efforts and the apparently little negative community reaction when we publicize our plans. Little do we realize that, in fact, the villagers are not at all taking kindly to the increased fees. This is shown quite clearly when one thousand local citizens march on the hospital demanding that our hospital administration be beaten and jailed.

That's not the outcome we'd expected. Another setback occurs when the Kampala-based NGO that has been advising us collapses and their advisors are pulled out of Uganda.

We are still convinced that some kind of health insurance scheme is necessary. Insurance will not only spare the family the burden of an overwhelming medical bill, but it will also encourage patients to seek medical care earlier in the course of an illness. Additionally, insurance will require BCH to be even more proactive in preventing disease.

In the search for other options, the model of a *Bataka* (burial) group is discussed. Burials are exceedingly expensive propositions in Uganda since hundreds of family members and friends arrive at the home of the deceased to comfort the bereaved. The ceremony lasts for days, and the family must provide food and drink for their guests during this time. *Batakas* were established in the mid-1980s during the AIDS epidemic. Death was rampant then and bodies lay around for extensive periods as relatives fervently searched for money for the burial. Some bodies were just discarded along the roadside.

This is how the idea of a *Bataka Twezikye* (natives, we bury ourselves) organization came into being—and remains today. A small amount of money is collected from villagers at the beginning of the year as a form of "death insurance." If you die during that year, your burial expenses are covered. The *Bataka* groups consist of as few as fifteen to twenty people or as many as several hundred individuals. The *Bataka* leaders, who control the money, are highly esteemed and trusted. They are not compensated for their service.

When we approach the *Bataka* leaders, they immediately appreciate the value of adding health insurance to death insurance and are willing to assist. It is agreed that 80 percent of the members of a *Bataka* group must join to prevent adverse selection whereby only the sickest patients enroll. The name the *Bataka* leaders choose for the insurance scheme is "*Bataka Twetambire*" (natives, we heal ourselves). The *Bataka* leaders sensitize the communities. As a result, many, many citizens descend on BCH, patiently waiting to register for the insurance. The entire Batwa population participates!

Long registration lines for eQuality Health Insurance

During the years of 2009 through 2010, more than thirty-five thousand individuals join at a cost of four dollars per person per year, with an eighty-cent copay at the time of service. It becomes one of the largest insurance plans with the best coverage in the country. The results are impressive, extending beyond simply improving access. Not only are our operating expenses less dependent on donations, but additionally, and even better, patients now seek health care earlier in the course of their illness. We find that hospital length of stays for those insured are markedly reduced, resulting in appreciable savings in the cost of delivering hospital care. Our research finds that death rates for children under the age of five are reduced over one-third among our insured population, at an expense of only four dollars per person per year! Access to quality health care now becomes an affordable option for one of the poorest areas of the world.

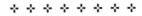

Although the insurance plan does save lives, death remains with us in a more visible way than in developed countries such as those in Europe or North America. Most medical students have never experienced a child dying in their arms, but this experience is common when they come to volunteer with us. A mechanism to process their grief is required. At our evening discussions, the most common question asked is, "How can a loving God allow so much suffering?" The discussions last long into the night.

When volunteers inquire how Ugandans deal with death, I mention a common phrase used at burials: *"Nentekateka ya Ruhanga,"* (it is the will of Ruhanga). A student asks if I believe that a child's death is ever God's will. I respond, "I believe in a God who is no stranger to suffering and who comforts us when we mourn. No, it would be hard for me to relate to a God who snatches away young kids, but I also realize that they and their families receive solace and reassurance believing that Ruhanga is in control."

One student who has recently cared for a dying child reflects, "Over the last four years of medical school, I have become quite proficient in the diagnosis and treatment of diseases, but I have received little instruction on how to comfort or provide compassion. I don't know the first thing about giving these people what they need in times like these."

Other students join in with profound insights:

"Sometimes, all you can do is hold a hand or offer an encouraging word."

"If I can connect with the patient, the illness might not be affected, but some sort of healing can take place, even if only in me."

Another student considers how this is affecting her own sense of who she is: "I think I'm learning who I am through helping others."

Many volunteers come to the Bwindi intent on changing the lives of the local people. After they return home and process the experience, they relate that it's their own lives and attitudes that have been transformed.

One such volunteer is Cara Skidgel.

We are not sure how to accommodate Cara. She's seventeen years old and lacks any medical training. She's a free spirit who is not used to supervision. I tell Cara that there are a few rules she must follow.

I point to the summit of a nearby ridge, the border between Uganda and the DRC. "Climbing that mountain and venturing into the Congo is not allowed. Lately, the rebels have been aggressive."

Cara does not want any part of Congolese rebels.

I add, "You need to sleep under a bed net. Even though we have medicines to treat malaria, malaria will make you miserable."

Cara says that she prefers avoiding misery.

"Finally, Cara, only drink filtered water, as the tap water may contain typhoid, among other deadly pathogens."

Cara seems comfortable with the guidelines and settles in for an experience that we hope will broaden her horizons.

Since Cara is interested in medicine, she spends many hours sitting in the wards, soaking up medical skills. She is especially drawn to children who are exceedingly ill.

Cara Skidgel delivering healthcare

Physicians typically develop protective mechanisms to insulate themselves from patients who are likely to die soon. I know myself well enough to notice that one of the ways I detach is to define the patient solely by their disease. For example, I talk about the child with cerebral malaria in bed two or the TB patient in isolation. They become objects of medical care rather than people who happen to have a disease.

As I am making rounds with several medical students, I stop at the bed of an adolescent who has a lethal heart condition. This child has been admitted with heart failure. After many days of treatment, he is still not responding. I presume that his death is imminent.

Cara is sitting on his bed. I greet Cara and tell the medical students that Cara is a high school student who has come to help. Continuing in my role as instructor, I have the students place their stethoscopes on the young man's chest then describe his heart defect in great detail. I conclude with, "Our medical regimen has not produced much improvement."

Cara interrupts and says, "His name is Fred, and he is very intelligent."

I mutter under my breath, "How callous of me to have not bothered to learn his name."

"And Fred can draw," notes Cara, as she points to several pictures of animals hanging around his bed.

As Fred talks about his artwork, a student notes, "Fred's quite the artist."

Another remarks, "He speaks English reasonably well."

I confess to Cara, "You have learned more about Fred than I've discovered in a week of being his physician."

During her stay, Cara supports the patients who are seriously ill. Her presence is therapeutic. In fact, day by day, Fred improves. As Fred leaves the hospital, he and Cara distribute his artwork to the kids in the pediatric ward.

Mother Teresa said, "We think that poverty is only being naked, hungry, and homeless, but the greatest form of poverty is being unwanted, unloved, and uncared for." Had I fallen into the trap of focusing so much on this child's medical condition that I failed to notice his need for human connection and genuine acknowledgement of his dignity as a person? Cara, through her gift of compassion, heals Fred's heart and opens mine.

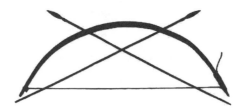

PART IV (2011 – 2017)

Partners in Health

"Sticks in a bundle are unbreakable."

—— • African Proverb • ——

CHAPTER 24

✧ ✧ ✧

The Batwa Take Charge
of Their Destiny

"Fear no forest because it is dense."

———— • African Proverb • ————

In our first decade of work with the Batwa, we emphasized address-ing their medical and educational needs. As we begin our second decade, we recognize that we need to be more sensitive to their social and cultural issues. The Batwa, outcasts from their ancient Bwindi Forest home, want to preserve the traditions and values that have formed them. When they were in the forest, they lived in clans: small, relatively independent family groups. They interacted with other clans when they gathered for a burial or a celebratory event. Now, living outside of the Bwindi Impenetrable Forest, they must frequently intermingle with other tribes as well as deal with the Ugandan government. Carol and I discuss how the Batwa can best organize themselves. Carol believes that if a solution is to be found, it will be through guidance from the Batwa. "It will be lots of fun," she adds.

When Carol and I meet with the Batwa at the village of Kitariro, they give a lively account of a recent trip to the local government office: "We have issues to discuss. To strengthen our spirits, we drink a lot of *tonto* (banana wine). It is a long walk to the government office. The office is confusing, but we find a person whose door is open. We surround him and make our demands; we pound on his desk, but he doesn't listen. He even seems frightened! What is his problem?"

Stifling our amusement, Carol suggests, "I think you might need to be more creative in your approach. The government can help you, but first you need to organize."

The Batwa ask, "What do you mean, organize?"

Carol patiently explains, "When you build a hut together, you have a common goal. What if all the settlements also work together for common goals?"

"What goals?" they ask.

Carol thinks for a while and responds, "We have been overseeing all of the projects; how about you managing them?"

"Do you mean the schools?" they ask.

Carol encourages them, "Yes, educating your children, and buying the land, and building the houses, and organizing the health care, and being responsible for the accounting."

"Accounting? Is that handling the money?" they enquire.

Carol smiles, "Yes, being responsible for the money."

This produces an animated discussion amongst them; we hear the word, *asente* (money) frequently repeated.

The Batwa are receptive. "Let's gather together elders from each settlement and discuss our problems and solutions."

Carol affirms, "Great idea, but will women be included?"

There is a pause. A Mutwa woman stands, pointing at the men, "Of course, we are the wisest!"

There is general laughter, and all agree that this is an excellent plan.

Over the course of six months, the Batwa of Kitariro collaborate with other Batwa settlements and agree that by organizing and working together, they can accomplish much. With some assistance from us, they form an NGO, naming it the Batwa Development Program (BDP). A committee composed exclusively of Batwa is in charge of the BDP. This committee is tasked with deciding which land to acquire, where homes will be built, which children will be educated, and who will talk to government officials. The future of the Batwa is in the hands of the BDP.

The BDP gathers for its initial meeting. Thirteen men and five women have been chosen as representatives from among the various settlements. We sit in a circle facing each other, sipping tea, warmed by the morning sun. The talk is lively. The Batwa elders have some familiarity with each other, but there is much to catch up on. The conversation revolves around relationships.

Pointing to a Mutwa nearby, one says, "I know you. Your father is Samuel. He is a great hunter with the bow."

Another comments, "Your mother, Ruth, she knows the legends of the forest and can sing."

"Ah, your cousin Kapere, he is a prankster. He covers himself in branches resembling a bush. Then he jumps out, terrifying folks walking on the trail." The Batwa howl, remembering Kapere's pranks.

After the pleasantries, they settle down to business. They decide that their leader should be a Mutwa named Benon. He's a handsome fellow with a ready smile. Benon lacks formal education but has an air of authority. It is obvious that Benon is in control—but of what? Interruptions are frequent and laughter common.

Benon thanks everyone for having confidence in him, "We have many problems that require attention, especially health and education."

"Our kids are not being treated well in school," a Mutwa complains.

"My kids don't like school."

"They don't like the food that is served in school."

"The Bakiga kids resent our kids studying with them."

Benon asks a hard question: "Are there ways that we can support the Bakiga kids? Don't you think that the Bakiga children have the same needs as our children?"

This produces an animated discussion and a few arguments:

"The Bakiga are not our friends," someone shouts.

"The Bakiga kick us out of the forest," moans another.

"All we do is fight with the Bakiga," says one, drawing back his fist in mock battle.

"The Bakiga own the land, we don't," asserts another.

"The Bakiga don't help us, so why should we help them?" an exasperated Batwa adds.

The meeting seems to be going nowhere until Benon quiets the room with this proverb, "*Abataine maino, Nagasan nibo aha enyama,*" (*Nagasan* gives meat to those who don't have teeth—meaning, essentially, that *Nagasan* does not discriminate).

The Batwa murmur their agreement.

He continues, "If the Batwa kids and Bakiga kids study together, they are friends."

More murmurs.

Benon sums it up with, "When we forgive them and work together, we are all better."

The arguments cease. Although there are obvious concerns, Carol tells the Batwa that she is moved by their understanding of forgiveness.

They are excited about this new venture in determining their own future. In further conversation, we find they are especially enthusiastic regarding the issue of money.

"How much money?"

"What can we do with it?"

"How much can we keep?"

The Batwa's lack of a future tense frustrates Carol's attempts to describe how money can be accumulated and used for future functions. She asks, "How will you pay for the next term's school fees?"

Their response centers only on their present needs:

"What about my children who are hungry and cry at night?"

"My house has no roof."

"My children have only rags to wear."

Carol agrees that there are challenges to be faced, but she suggests that the BDP is a good place to start. She then points out that there are consequences to their having authority. "There can be problems with making decisions. What about a Mutwa child running away from school, or a Batwa family not using the land well, or someone misusing the money?"

Their joy is muted as they ask, "You are assisting, aren't you?"

Carol nods, "Of course we'll help, but this is a learning process, and mistakes are great teachers."

They aren't pleased with the prospect of facing bad decisions or mistakes, but the opportunity of controlling the money is particularly attractive. They also understand that as their children become educated in finances, health, and education, they will be the leaders.

At a later BDP gathering, the Batwa are very animated discussing the outcome of a meeting with a government official. They claim, "The officials listen to us!"

"Why?" I ask.

"We meet beforehand to discuss our problems and who talks at the meeting. Oh, and we decide no drinking *tonto*," they chuckle.

The Batwa are beginning to work together and speak with one voice. In addition, they're getting results.

I tell them that there is a very wise, diminutive Indian lady, probably not much taller than them, named Mother Teresa. She says, "I can do things that you cannot, you can do things that I cannot, but together we can do great things."

"Will she join the BDP?" they shout.

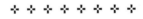

At one of the BDP's first meetings, Carol talks about the value of educating their children. She begins, "You need Batwa teachers, Batwa accountants, Batwa nurses, and Batwa managers. Your kids must attend school."

The Batwa listen patiently but are unusually quiet and seem dejected.

Carol asks, "Please tell me, what is the problem?"

They answer, "Education in schools run by Bakiga is fine, but don't we Batwa have anything to teach our own children?"

Carol and I are surprised by this comment. Had we forgotten to consider the Batwa as educators themselves?

Carol gently asks, "What do you want to teach your children?"

"We want to teach our children about life in the forest."

"It is necessary that our children love the forest, not fear it like the Bakiga."

"We must teach them our legends."

"Our children need to learn our songs and our dances."

"What prevents you from teaching them these things?" Carol inquires.

"The teaching can only be done in the forest."

Carol explains to the Batwa, "Your original forest is not accessible, it's under the control of the Ugandan government. Almost all the land outside of the Bwindi Impenetrable Forest has been deforested for agriculture. What little patches of forest land remain are controlled by a few landowners, and none are willing to sell. But we'll search. Can we agree that if we find a forest for you to teach your children your songs, dances, and legends, you will send your kids to school?"

The Batwa shout their agreement with the compromise.

I express my concern to Carol about our ability to fulfill our commitment, but Carol reassures me, "God has provided for us all along. Don't worry, just have patience."

Several months later, Stephen, a local Mukiga, arrives at our house. We invite him to join us for lunch. Over simple fare of matoke, beans, and rice, Stephen says he's heard of the BDP and that the Batwa need land. After lunch, he asks us to accompany him to a vantage point near our house. He points to where the Bwindi Impenetrable

Forest is surrounded by denuded agricultural terrain. The contrast is sharp; a dense, verdant green abutting pale, brown fields. "Do you see that area of the forest that sticks out into the millet fields?" We observe with Stephen that there is a large chunk of the forest that juts out from the straight line of the demarcation between forest and agricultural land. "I own this land; it is over one hundred acres and is the only remaining privately owned forested parcel in this region."

Stephen continues, "I do have an interested buyer; he is a relative."

Carol enquires, "What will your relative do with the property?"

Stephen responds, "He plans to cut the forest to plant millet."

Carol is devastated. She exclaims, "Millet??" Speaking more calmly she adds, "Your forest is an area where the mountain gorillas forage."

Stephen continues, "I know that the gorillas come to my land. I prefer that the Batwa own it; they will preserve and protect it."

Reluctantly, Carol inquires, "How much?"

Stephen flatly states, "My relative will pay me $25,000."

I murmur, "That kind of money just isn't in our budget."

Carol pulls me aside and reminds me, "Honey, we recently sold a one-third acre property in California for just over $25,000. Don't you think this is a good exchange, one-third acre for one hundred acres?"

We ask Stephen to return in the morning.

As soon as Stephen departs, I gather several BDP elders and we hike up through cleared agricultural and grazing land. The Batwa wander about, seeming disoriented until they arrive at a wall of dense trees. This is Stephen's land. Hanging vines, protruding roots, and fallen trees impede my progress. Here, the Batwa seem to come alive; their talk becomes more muted, they move in a fluid, purposeful fashion, at one with the forest.

They excitedly tell me, "Before, this is our hunting land."

As we hike upward, they recognize a large overhanging rock. "This is where we build fires to dry the meat when we kill animals."

Higher up the slope, they huddle under a vertical cliff with a naturally carved out area at the base. "This is where our elders offer sacrifices to *Nabingi*."

They stop frequently along the way to point out several of their medicinal plants. "These plants only grow in the forest."

This forest is a true gift!

The next day, Stephen returns and we conclude the sale. Stephen signs, government officials sign, and the Batwa BDP elders proudly place their inked thumbprints on the document. Banana wine is liberally shared and there is high-spirited singing and dancing. The land is now returned to the original inhabitants, the Batwa and the mountain gorillas.

Overjoyed to regain a portion of their homeland, the Batwa eagerly set about the task of building a village, house by house. Using sticks, they form a simple, inverted, conical frame, around six feet across at its base, like a native American tepee. They then weave grass and leaves between the branches. After several hours of work, a compact, water-resistant structure is completed that will accommodate a family of four. Over the course of a few weeks, they construct a traditional forest settlement consisting of eight houses, each structure nestled against a rock or tree for added protection. This village arises as a seamless part of the environment.

The Batwa name the place "Batwa *Okuguubwaho*," which is loosely translated as "Batwa Experience." The Batwa *Okuguubwaho* will allow the Batwa to teach their children the life and lore of the forest. At the Batwa *Okuguubwaho*, their rich cultural traditions will be treasured. It's living history.

Several Batwa elders are chosen as instructors. These elders know the forest. They have grown up learning the ancestral lore, the songs, the dances. They have a thorough knowledge of medicinal plants and understand the spirit of the forest. Each week, groups of eight to ten

Batwa children spend two days in this "living classroom" where the elders instruct them in their heritage.

On a Friday afternoon, I pick up a group of Batwa kids from school. We drive to the end of a road and hike up the steep ridge. When we enter the forest, the children seem rather disoriented, particularly when bark cloth clad elders suddenly emerge, gaily drumming, dancing, and singing. The elders lead the kids up a narrow trail, stopping periodically to explain how they set traps for small game, where yams can be found, and how the stems of certain plants, when cut, are a source for water. After an hour's walk, we emerge from the forest into a clearing. Simple huts are scattered about, smoke curling from the roofs. Batwa women busy themselves weaving baskets while young children snuggle at their breasts.

The scene is an inspiring and timeless one. It seems to harken to a time when humankind lived as one with the environment, having a profound reverence for nature. Their faces clearly reflect a joy at being home again. It is a gift to be a participant in their forest life.

One recently completed structure is a tree house "duplex" consisting of two inconspicuous shelters constructed one on top of the other in the branches of a large tree. Several Batwa children scamper up a strong vine ladder to the tree lodges. Before they enter, a Batwa elder restrains them, quickly

Batwa Experience

rapping his stick around the inside of the hut, telling the startled kids, "*Watina enzoka*," (You should fear snakes). "One never enters a tree lodge without first banging a stick to chase away any snakes, especially the black mamba."

At the mention of black mamba, the kids shrink back.

The students are amazed by the elders who can make fire by rubbing sticks together. A diminutive elderly woman, Nora, shows the kids her abode hollowed out under a large tree. "This is where my husband and I curl up for the night."

Nora at home

I overhear a young Batwa say to his friend, "I'm not sure that I like it here. I miss my mattress and pillow."

As I depart, the elders instruct the youths regarding using bows and arrows and traps. I tell the kids that I will pick them up on Sunday.

Two days later, I meet the kids as they emerge from the forest. They are all smiles, gaily talking about the excitement of life in the forest. They tease each other regarding how they worried about spending a night here. Now they are repeating the legends that they have been told and sharing their amazing forest adventures. They relish their history.

Over several months, the Batwa Experience matures and tourists express interest in visiting the site. On an overcast day with a wispy mist from a recent rain hanging over the Bwindi, I hike to the Batwa Experience with several visitors. James, the elderly Mutwa hunter, leads the tour. Along the way, James points out herbs that are therapeutic for a variety of conditions: curing fevers, malaria, diarrhea, skin conditions, and parasites.

One herb James handles carefully. "This is used when relations between husband and wife are difficult due to inattention by the husband. The remedy for this dilemma is preparing a fine meal for the injured spouse and adding a portion of the herb to the food. When

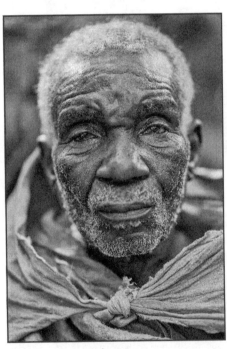

James

the partner consumes the herb, she forgives her husband and immediately becomes passionate. I use this plant. It works!"

James then shows the tourists an interesting rock structure. "Here is where we offer sacrifices to our god *Nabingi*. We fear *Nabingi*, as he produces fevers, sickness, and even death. We are thankful that *Nagasan* cares for us and protects us from *Nabingi*, but every day we offer gifts to *Nabingi*."

A tourist asks, "Why is there fruit and banana wine in that crevice?"

James, smiling broadly, responds, "These are offered to *Nabingi*, but we come nightly and gather whatever *Nabingi* does not consume and have a party. *Nabingi* must not be very hungry."

James then takes the visitors into the forest, demonstrating the traps and snares that the Batwa use to catch animals.

He is asked, "Did you hunt the gorillas?"

James is emphatic. "We Batwa never hunt the mountain gorilla or chimpanzee. We also have a taboo against eating *enzoka* (snake)."

Suddenly, in the forest above, a great commotion is heard, and James exclaims, "Come quickly, a forest duiker (a small bush antelope) is spotted. The hunt is on!" He gives me a wink as we race up the steep slope.

A Mutwa motions with his hand for us to halt, he points to a carved wooden duiker skillfully hidden in the underbrush. Silently, he pulls the bowstring taut and releases the arrow. When it accurately strikes the target, the Batwa cheer in unison.

The Batwa suspend the wooden duiker from a pole, and we join in the gay procession back to the village. When we arrive, the women break into a traditional hunting song and a vigorous dance, expressing joy over the hunt's success.

Eager to test the *bazungu's* archery skills, the Batwa set up carved wooden animals as targets. One *muzungu* mentions that he is proficient in archery. To the embarrassment of his friends, he suggests a competition: Batwa against *bazungu*. Smiling at the opportunity to demonstrate their abilities, the Batwa focus, skillfully draw back the bow, and send the arrows to their mark. They hand the bows and arrows to the tourist, "It's your turn."

As several tourists miss widely, James chuckles, "It is apparent that surviving in the forest might be difficult for you."

The last to shoot is the *muzungu* who initiated the contest. He handles the bow deftly, pulls the string nearly to its breaking point, and lets the arrow fly. The arrow strikes the target and the Batwa erupt in wild applause and congratulations. Pleased with his accuracy, he questions James, "Why are you cheering for me? I thought that we were competing against one another."

James patiently explains, "In the hunt, we must work together, or else we go hungry. When one does well, we all benefit. When one suffers, we all suffer. Isn't it the same in your country?"

After considering the question, the tourist answers, "We in the U.S. commonly use the expression 'United We Stand,' but we value our self-reliance and our individualism. It is obvious that working together brings out the best in people. We in the West need to do more of this."

The Batwa murmur their agreement.

Before the tourists depart, all join in for one last dance, a traditional dance of giving thanks. Judging from their smiles, the tourists are learning to enjoy the forest.

As we descend the mountain, I notice that one *muzungu* has a few herbs protruding from his backpack.

When I inquire, he whispers with a grin, "Let's just say I need to prepare a meal for my wife."

CHAPTER 25

✤ ✤ ✤

Strong Women, Woven Together

"When spider webs unite, they can tie up a lion."

━━ · African Proverb · ━━

The results of the BDP's collaborations are successful enough that additional Batwa communities join the organization. One of the most remote settlements and newest member of the BDP is Nteko.

I join a few BDP elders and two friends from the U.S., Steve Gonsalves and Richard Cunningham, on a hike through the Bwindi Impenetrable Forest to reach Nteko. Steve and I have become close friends. Steve previously worked in Hollywood as an actor. He has a brilliant smile, a hearty disposition, and seems unfazed by any tribulation. Steve initially arrived with a Rotary group for a two-week service trip. His personality resonated with the people and local culture, and, as he was at a transition point in his life, he decided to stay. Now, four years later, he is having "the best time of my life!"

As we enter the mist-shrouded forest, the light dims and the temperature drops. The immensity of the dense foliage, the ferns, the low-lying moss, and the towering trees overwhelm us. An amazing collection of brilliantly colored birds chatters from the canopy.

Richard is in his seventies and is amazingly fit. He seems to glide along the trail. I ask if he has ever run competitively. He tells me, "I set the NCAA indoor record for the mile—just over four minutes."

He then explains how he became engaged with the Batwa and started his weaving project.

"I have always been fascinated by wildlife. My wife Katie and I came to trek the gorillas. It was a wonderful experience; however, I found that the people living next to the park were poor and hungry. We particularly noticed that the women wove striking baskets. I believed that, with some modifications, their baskets could be sold for a substantial price. Although I had no prior experience with weaving, in collaboration with the ladies, we formed an organization named the Virunga Artisans. We have been selling the baskets in the U.S. and returning the profits to them."

Grinning, he remarks, "This helps them feed their families and prevents poaching in the forest—and Katie and I get to come back here often. We love it here!"

After eight hours of hiking, we arrive in Nteko. Richard presents the Batwa with a drum, and then he and Steve amaze the Batwa with energetic dance steps. At sunset, we collect around a campfire. Eyes flicker in the firelight as stories and tales are exchanged. For a moment, I feel part of this forest and this Batwa tribe, sharing in a civilization that stretches back thousands of years. The stars twinkle above. As the earth cools below, the fire warms and unites us. We have been included intimately in the lives of the Batwa. The Batwa gradually retire to their huts and we to our tents as the fire dies.

In the morning, I walk through the village and see the impact of the basket weaving program. The Batwa live in sturdy houses and have deep pit latrines, clean water catchment systems, and improved gardens.

Over the next few days, Richard and I visit different groups where, several times a week, women weave together. It is apparent that they have formed tight relationships.

At each group, Richard motivates the women to continually improve the quality of their baskets through tighter weaves, innovative patterns, and judicious use of the natural dyes. These women appreciate Richard's input and commitment.

After one of these meetings, I casually talk with the women. They remind me of a previous visit: "I saw many of you years ago. Some of you had bruises on your arms and faces. I was concerned about you; alcohol was prevalent in your community and your children were not being educated."

"Yes, those times are difficult," they agree.

"It must be better now. You are so beautifully dressed. And you are carrying purses. You tell me your kids are attending school. I see only happy faces! What has changed?"

"We have money from selling our baskets in America."

"But you had money before, from digging in the field. I know that your husbands often took your money to spend on alcohol. What happened to the drinking?"

In unison, the women respond, "Our husbands cannot take our money and use it to get drunk."

"Why not?"

"While we weave, we talk, and if a husband is rowdy or takes our money, we'll talk with him."

"What happens if he doesn't listen?"

"Then we return as a group and beat him!"

I try not to show my shock.

I persist, "What happens if one of your members has bruises inflicted by an abusive husband?"

Again, in unison they shout, "We put the same bruises on him!"

"We are happy now. We know how to support ourselves and each other."

These women have become resilient, taking pride in themselves and their work. They have a strong sense of dignity and group identity.

Retracing our steps through the forest, I tell Richard how impressed I am with the weavers' group that he and Katie have started. I'm stunned that a small-enterprise program has resulted in such profound social changes.

Richard is thrilled that I recognize the same changes he and Katie are seeing. He says, "The ladies of Nteko and the weavers' groups have a bright future. Together, they are not only weaving beautiful baskets but also knitting their lives together."

CHAPTER 26

✤ ✤ ✤

A Healing Partnership

"Ordinary people are as common as grass,
but good people are dearer than the eye."

———— • African Proverb • ————

With a traditional Western scientific background, I have been reluctant for years to engage with an important segment of the local healing community, the *abafumu*, who are frequently visited by both the Batwa and the Bakiga. *Abafumu* are practitioners of traditional medicine; they are perhaps better known as "medicine men." Each tribal group have *abafumu*. They are highly respected by all— except me. They take an approach to healing so vastly different from my Western approach that I believe working with them is impossible.

This changes with one visit. One evening, we welcome my fellow Tulane medical graduate, Ken, along with his daughter, Kristen, a bright, inquisitive medical student. They have had a long journey from Kampala. Despite the arduous trip, they are in good spirits. Ken is interested in alternative medical practices and preventive medicine. He plans to spend his time assessing traditional methods for treating and preventing disease.

Several weeks later, Ken suggests that we meet to discuss the results of his research. Sitting on the porch with Ken and Kristen as the morning rays warm us, Ken begins by asking me a difficult question, "I have been talking with the *abafumu*. How do you relate to them?"

I am aware that Ken has noticed the tension between the *abafumu* and me. I admit, "This is a thorny issue. Relations are not good. I think of the *abafumu* more as witchdoctors; however, the Batwa highly regard their herbal remedies. The *abafumu* treat the Batwa with respect and they return that respect. I have no issue with using herbs as medical treatment; I've witnessed their effectiveness. One of their plants successfully induces labor, another reduces fever, and many men swear by the improved potency derived from another."

Kristen adds, "Many medicines that we use in the U.S. are plant derivatives."

As we sip our tea, I express my main reservations. "Yes, but there are some practices that I consider cruel and unethical. The *abafumu* use *okuhanduura oburo* (cutting the skin), for a variety of illnesses. This process involves making cuts in the skin and placing medicinal herbs in the incisions, quickly producing festering cuts...." I pause for a moment, then continue,

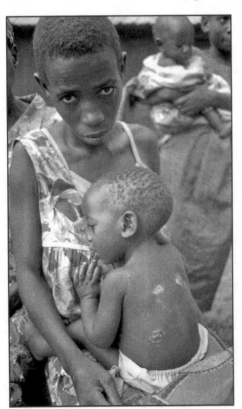
The indigenous practice of kwosya

"Even more difficult for me to fathom is the practice called *kwosya,* where hot, brand-like implements are applied over a diseased area to draw out the infection. Children arrive at our hospital with multiple second-degree burns. If pneumonia is the problem, then the child typically has burns over the chest; if prolonged diarrhea, then they are branded over the abdomen. I can tell at a glance what the *omufumu* (singular form of *abafumu*) is thinking by the location and age of the burns.

"The practice that troubles me most is the removal of teeth. When I first arrived at the Bwindi, I was perplexed when I found that many young children were missing their lower canine teeth. I learned that the *abafumu* had a custom of extracting the lower incisors, a practice they call *ebino* or *kukura ameno*. When maternal antibodies wane, young children frequently develop mild infections. This coincides with the timing of the eruption of the lower canine tooth buds. The *abafumu* apparently associate the two, thinking that the tooth buds are the cause of the infections. So they yank them out."

Ken interjects, "I wondered why many of the kids were lacking these teeth."

"It's more than just the loss of teeth; occasionally there are consequences far more serious. Since nonsterile wire or bicycle spokes are used for the extractions, some kids develop infections, tetanus, or HIV, and some even die. In the medical literature, this practice is labeled Infant Oral Mutilation."

Ken and Kristen are shocked.

"How can I have a relationship with *abafumu* who subject seriously ill children to cuttings, burnings, and tooth extraction?"

Ken pauses and reflects before he answers, "I agree with your view about these particular practices. However, in my research, at least 90 percent of your patients have been seen by an *omufumu* before they come to your hospital. You feel that you cannot work with them, but in reality, you can't work without them."

I consider this new perspective, flabbergasted.

Ken recalls a quote from Hippocrates: "Wherever the art of medicine is loved, there is also the love of humanity."

Kristen prods me, "Perhaps if you meet with the *abafumu*, you will find common ground."

Accepting Ken's suggestion, I make a request to an *omufumu* acquaintance that I would like to meet with his fellow practitioners.

He offers, "Perhaps you are willing to meet with them, but they might not want to meet with you."

"I understand that. But let's give it a go!" A message is sent setting a day to meet, but I receive no reply. Yet, on the appointed day, I hear drumming in the distance. Around forty *abafumu* drift into our house, many dressed in traditional garb. I am intimidated by some of the sinister-looking outfits. I relax somewhat when I recognize several friends who are part of this healing group. We distribute warm sodas, freshly baked bread, and fruit as we gather shoulder to shoulder in our living room.

Nabingi

After we are seated, introductions proceed. Each *omufumu* rises and states his or her name and particular area of expertise. I am amazed by their specialization: some concentrate on the treatment of malaria, while others on pneumonia or poisonings or lightning strikes. Others focus on marital discord, many announcing that their potency remedies are efficacious. Most are versed in the casting and removal of spells.

When it is my turn to speak, I discuss my interest in diseases of the tropics and public health. The group seems genuinely intrigued.

I then inquire, "Do you have any concerns about meeting with me?"

One elderly *omufumu*, whose specialty is restoration of potency and casting spells, rises. He has an air of authority. Exuding malice, he states, "We believe that you disrespect us and what we practice!"

I am confused but respond sincerely, "I have trouble understanding your traditions. If you consider me judgmental, I am sorry. I will try to keep an open mind."

The *omufumu* then points a bony finger at me, raises his voice, and puts me on the spot, "We all want to know what you think about our practices of *kwosya* (burning), *okuhanduura oboro* (cutting), and *ebino* (forcibly extracting teeth)."

I am bewildered and do not know how to reply, as these are the three practices most troubling for me. Nevertheless, I'm aware that a negative answer will threaten our relationship and immediately terminate the meeting. Trapped, I search for an appropriate response.

During the prolonged silence, a spectral form slowly arises in the rear of the room. Features are almost unrecognizable: a shawl is covering the head; deep-set eyes seem to glow from a darkened face. The frame is encased in a traditional dark weaving; I can just barely identify it as the frame of a woman. Her only distinguishing features are jewelry on her fingers and supple hands grasping a cane. Although her body is stooped from arthritis, she rises easily and seems to float rather than walk. She has an aura of intense power.

The man next to me whispers in my ear, "That's Batusa!"

The hair rises on the back of my neck and my heart races. I have heard about Batusa for many years. She is the most respected and powerful of all the *abafumu*. Her spells reportedly have great effect and can result in life or death. I've seen the consequences of her curses, having admitted extremely ill patients to our hospital who claimed to be dying due to Batusa's curse. Despite what remedies I administered, they would too frequently waste away.

Batusa throws back her head scarf and fixes her gaze on me. I visibly shrink back, but I detect a subtle grin at the edge of her lips. She slowly glides over to the fellow grilling me. She places her hands on his shoulders and, looking directly into his face, she gently but firmly forces him down into his chair.

Batusa pauses, and then faces the group.

In a commanding voice, she announces, "We will not be talking about our differences. We will only talk about what we have in common!"

After she lets this message sink in, she continues, "What we have in common is improving the health of our people."

Her smile widens as she approaches me. "This is a good man who is dedicating his time to the care of our community. We must work with him."

From this moment on, Batusa and I become linked in a bond of friendship and cooperation. With Batusa's wise counsel, many divisive issues will be resolved.

We adjourn outside, accompanied by a resounding drumbeat, all joining in joyous singing and dancing. As we return to the meeting for more tea and bread, I consider the previous week, which has been particularly bad for malaria cases. Three patients, two infants, and a pregnant mother had been initially treated by the *abafumu*. By the time they arrived at our facility, it was too late, and they succumbed from malaria. I look for an opportunity to raise this concern.

Surprisingly, it's the *abafumu* themselves who first speak of malaria.

"Will you teach us about *omuswiija* (malaria)?"

"Our remedies are not successful; too many children are dying."

"Even our own children die," they lament.

"We must know more about *omuswiija*."

We agree that at the next meeting we will tackle malaria.

Before departing, one *omufumu* pulls me aside and expresses his gratitude for the opportunity to talk. Apparently, he had been reticent to approach me for fear of being criticized. Now he notes, "The *abafumu* and *muzungu* doctor are sitting together, sharing food, and discussing how to improve the health of our community."

An eagerness to learn from one another results in a plan to meet monthly. We look forward to new and exciting collaborations. I now understand that all healers, whether trained in a medical school or in the art of spells and curses are bound together through a love of humanity.

At dinner, Carol and I reflect on the day's events. Once again, we've seen how disagreements at the Bwindi and elsewhere can be resolved by the sharing of bread, careful listening, and focusing on common interests instead of differences. Carol wishes that politicians would follow this example, and she makes a generous offer: "I'll be glad to supply the bread and drums!"

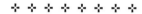

Months later, we are taking stock of the progress of our work over the past year. As we consider the earlier part of the year, we notice more downs than ups: our Land Rover seemed on the verge of extinction; during their periodic inspections, Ugandan officials have been prickly with us; we had some misunderstandings with the Batwa; and we recall feeling exhausted and ready for a break. However, over the last few months, things seem different: our bond with the Batwa seems tighter than ever, our Land Rover is running smoothly, and Carol and I are again experiencing joy in our work.

On a walk, I pass by a group of Bakiga elders congregating under a tree. They invite me to join. I remove my backpack and sit on a wobbly rock. They discuss the concerns of the day, like who is in trouble, who has a drinking issue, and local political dynamics. I hear snatches of conversations regarding who is pregnant and speculations of who could be the father—all accompanied by laughter and amusement.

Then they turn their attention to me:

"How is the hospital?"

"How is your wife, Carol?"

"How are you faring?"

I thank them for their concern and say that all is well. I conclude, "It was difficult a while back; we had many problems. But now our work is going well, and Carol and I are very happy."

One of the elders responds in an inquisitive manner: "When did you recognize that things had changed?"

I hadn't thought about a time frame, but, taking my journal from my backpack and rummaging through months of entries, I tell the elders, "It appears that our lives started improving early last spring."

The elders smile, looking at one another. One continues, "Was it around the time when you started meeting with the *abafumu*?"

Rechecking my journal entries, I respond, "Why, yes, it was."

The elders poke each other and roar with laughter, seemingly at my expense. Recovering from the amusement, an elderly fellow states, "Don't you know the reason for the change?"

"No, but I'd love to know," I reply, somewhat confused.

Another interjects, "Don't you realize that the *abafumu* removed the curse that they had placed on you?"

"A curse?" I respond in bewilderment.

Then I hear, "For years, the *abafumu* did not like you; they feared you and felt threatened by you. They had been placing curses on you."

Another adds, "You were a threat to their income and reputation. It is not good to anger the *abafumu*."

"Now the *abafumu* realize that you have a common cause and that you are a friend whom they can trust. The evening after that first meeting at your house, Batusa had them gather on a hilltop, performing an all-night ceremony to remove their curses."

I agree with the elders that it is not good to anger the *abafumu*.

When I relate this conversation to Carol, she is somewhat dubious about the power of curses, but she agrees that we should stay in the good graces of the *abafumu*. "They're certainly fun to be with. And they are the best dancers!"

CHAPTER 27

✤ ✤ ✤

Malaria Struck Down,
and Doctor Struck Out

"If you think that you are too small to make a difference,
you haven't spent the night with a mosquito."

———— • African Proverb • ————

When the *abafumu* crowd into our living room for our monthly meeting, they are animated and lively. Carol receives hugs and thanks for providing bread, fruit, tea, and a welcoming environment. The conversations are upbeat and spirited.

I introduce Luke McDonald. Luke is an intelligent, fit, and dedicated student who is attending Tulane medical school on a Navy scholarship. Luke tells the *abafumu* about his interest in diseases of the tropics. The *abafumu* seem pleased with Luke's knowledge and willingness to engage.

My language skills remain a challenge; they smile at my attempts, evidently appreciating my efforts to communicate in their native tongue. I remind them that we have agreed to work together to prevent and successfully treat *omuswiija* (malaria). We gather in a circle, and I relate the circumstances of a recently admitted child with *omuswiija*. Motioning toward Luke, I continue: "Luke inserted an IV and gave medication for seizures. Blood was transfused and the child seemed to improve. However, the child suddenly has a seizure. The breathing became irregular."

Speaking through one of our Makiga interpreters, Luke picks up the narrative and demonstrates how the child's breathing slows and then ceases. He drops his arms in frustration: "The child dies."

The *abafumu* nod; they understand death.

Luke continues, "The next day, as we attend the burial ceremony at the mother's village, friends and relatives crowd around the tiny body. Their singing and sharing lifts our spirits."

The *abafumu* speak among themselves recalling similar experiences with children dying of malaria and attending burials. "We have an expression, *'Nitushemererwa hamwe kandi nitushasha hamwe.'* We think that the closest *muzungu* equivalent is 'Shared joy is double joy, and shared grief is half grief.'"

I agree. "Sharing our adversities and our successes has allowed Carol and me to remain in Africa. Sharing is a gift to us."

I turn the meeting over to Luke. He begins by explaining that records indicate malaria has afflicted people for nearly five thousand years. "The word malaria originated from 'mal' (bad) 'aira' (air) since people believed that it was caused by the vapors from swamps. There is no vaccine. Malaria causes 1.2 million deaths worldwide. Almost all these deaths are in sub-Saharan African children, most under the age of five. Every thirty seconds, a child dies from malaria."

The *abafumu* murmur among themselves.

I mention that our efforts to distribute mosquito netting to prevent malaria have failed. Many villagers refuse to accept nets, as they believe that *omuswiija* is due to *Stan* (St-aan – a demon).

At the mention of *Stan*, the tenor of the conversation shifts and becomes more intense and reverential.

I tell the *abafumu*, "I am confused. What does *Stan* have to do with *omuswiija*?"

Batusa firmly states, "Because *Stan* causes *omuswiija*."

Luke seems particularly perplexed, "*Stan*? What is *Stan*?"

Batusa quietly continues, "*Stan* is a god of our ancestors. After the death of a relative, if adequate sacrifices are not made, then *Stan* returns to cause all kinds of illnesses, especially *omuswiija*. *Stan* is very powerful; he is not to be annoyed."

Luke inquires, "Why do you believe that *Stan* causes *omuswiija*?"

"Because, when young children have *omuswiija*, they shake about with seizures. They are obviously possessed by a demon. It is *Stan*."

Another *omufumu* states with conviction, "A net cannot prevent *Stan* from attacking children. *Stan* slips right through."

Luke and I confer, Luke suggests that we demonstrate *omuswiija* to the *abafumu*.

He asks the *abafumu*, "Have you ever seen *omuswiija*?"

They shake their heads no and look confused.

"Come with me, I'll show you," Luke says.

We take the *abafumu* to the hospital laboratory where we request lab technicians to teach the *abafumu* about *omuswiija*. The lab techs eagerly describe the malaria parasite as seen through a microscope. They encourage the *abafumu* to peer through the lens, telling them, "Look to where the eyepiece cursor is pointing. You see circular red blood cells with small parasite dots inside them."

"Can you see them?" the lab tech queries.

One after another they nod. "Yes, I see them."

"That's the culprit, *omuswiija* damages red blood cells and causes the kids to be anemic," the lab tech affirms.

Next, we visit the children's ward where mothers lie in beds next to their children being treated for malaria.

Standing next to a comatose child, Luke

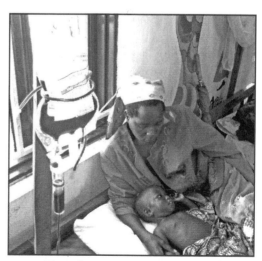

Transfusing an anemic child suffering from malaria

tells the *abafumu*, "This is how we treat malaria. There are two IVs. Through one IV, we give the child blood to correct the anemia; the other IV is infusing quinine to treat the malaria. Although, it is much better to prevent this disease than to treat it."

The *abafumu* agree that *omuswiija* is best prevented.

Back in our meeting room at the hospital guest house, several medical students display drawings of the life cycle of the anopheles mosquitos and how they transmit *omuswiija*. They describe, with animated mosquito buzzing sounds and the "ouch" of the bite, the life cycle of malaria in the human and the mosquito. The *abafumu* are very attentive.

Eventually, the *abafumu* agree that the mosquito is the perpetrator and that bed nets are useful in the prevention of *omuswiija*.

I tell the *abafumu*, "We have obtained an inexpensive source for bed nets. We can provide them at no charge."

This announcement fails to have the effect I am hoping for. Batusa speaks up adamantly, "Your plan has no chance for success!"

"Why?" I ask.

Batusa asserts, "If the nets are to be valued, then the people must contribute."

Another adds, "Bed nets, which are given at no cost, are used as dresses and for catching small fish."

The medical students are incredulous that the mosquito nets are not being used as intended. They are even more adamant concerning the cost involved. "In my country, it is not proper to charge a poor person for something that can prevent their child from dying."

Batusa insists, "Unless something is contributed, the nets are not prized or used correctly."

Reluctantly, we agree with their plan. The *abafumu* agree that a reasonable price for a bed net is 2,500 Uganda shillings (one dollar), but a bow, an arrow, or a basket can also be used as payment. The *abafumu* help organize the villagers by speaking at public meetings and schools, explaining the necessity of using bed nets.

Several government officials and NGOs learn of our plan requiring payment for the nets. They complain to me: "Americans have donors who can help our poor African children. Why is there a charge?"

I explain, "This plan was developed by the *abafumu*; the fee demonstrates the value of the netting. And, besides, bows and arrows are acceptable payment, and we don't think most Americans are willing to contribute archery equipment."

The *abafumu* help us identify the most vulnerable: children under the age of five and pregnant mothers. We are determined that all these non-immune individuals should be provided with a net. Our net campaign launches, and the response is surprising. Our net sales quickly increase to over one thousand per month. After two years, we've distributed over thirty thousand nets. The result is a substantial drop in the admission rates for malaria at the Bwindi Community Hospital and a marked reduction in the number of outpatient cases.

We celebrate this wonderful, small victory over malaria with a party for the *abafumu*. My spirits soar as I compliment them on their efforts: "The majority of children in our area are sleeping under bed nets. Three years ago, Bwindi Community Hospital's records indicated that one to two children were dying of *omuswiija* every week. Over the last nine months, not one child has died from *omuswiija*!"

The *abafumu* cheer as one affirms, "Now, I rarely see children with *omuswiija*."

Another shouts, "And my kids are also sleeping under bed nets and are not sick with *omuswiija*!"

When the cheering subsides, I inform the *abafumu*, "*Omuswiija* has been reduced by over 90 percent. Malaria has not been completely defeated, but children now survive because of the use of bed nets."

"Bed nets AND the support and cooperation of the *abafumu*," Batusa adds.

The *abafumu* cheer again.

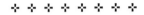

Our friendly relationships with the *abafumu* have lifted our spirits. Progress with the Batwa, as well as relief from all the administrative duties of the hospital, have restored our enjoyment of life at the Bwindi. My friend Dr. Birungi, a wonderful and dedicated Ugandan doctor, is now the hospital's superintendent. Our lives have been calm for quite some time.

Board members of the Kellermann Foundation periodically join us from the U.S. to support us and view the progress of the projects. I have learned they will be arriving soon, so I travel to Kampala to meet them. Kampala is always a shock to the senses after the bucolic life of the Bwindi. A profusion of chirps from colorful birds and the chatter of monkeys in the dense forest are exchanged for the blaring of horns, snarled traffic, and a tumultuous mass of humanity.

One must be careful in Kampala. I am ever vigilant, carrying only a backpack containing my laptop computer, a camera, cell phone, and my journal. I also have money hidden in a secret pants pocket. I take refuge from the chaos at a small restaurant overlooking the traffic and pedestrians below. I reflect on the privilege of using my talents in this fascinating part of the world, working with such interesting and engaging people. Tears flow easily. With a satisfied stomach and a light heart, I walk to the mission guest house.

Then lightning strikes.

I awake and, though blurred vision, I view a surgical mask and cap framing two eyes that are intently staring at me. The smell of alcohol fills the air.

My foggy brain realizes that this can't be good. I don't know where I am. I feel like I've been through a trash compactor. There's blood in my mouth and I have a splitting headache. My tongue probes the ragged geography of my shattered front teeth. The fellow in the surgical mask is holding a huge, curved surgical needle, while he approaches my face. This is really not good. I'd love to pass it off as a nightmare.

The needle wielding medic tells me, "You are in the emergency room of Mengo Hospital in Kampala. You are okay, except that your face has been rearranged. Just relax."

Relax? Really?

He continues the narrative: "Thieves snuck up on you. They hit you on the back of the head with an iron bar and struck you in the face. You were out cold. They robbed you, tossed you in a ditch, and left you for dead. Someone found you and dropped you off here."

The young medic seems more eager to repair my facial lacerations than to talk. Through my fog, I ask, "What type of suture are you using?"

"Number 2 is all that I have."

"Hey, that's more like rope. Maybe something finer? And any chance of locating a surgeon?"

He continues, "You should consider yourself lucky. Your face got messed up, but we see many victims, similarly assaulted. We just transfer them to the morgue. As to finer suture material, we're out of stock."

I've heard that one before.

It's very hard for me to feel lucky, but I agree that it's better to require stitches rather than wear a toe tag. With some apprehension, I ask to look in a mirror. With nurses supporting me, I limp to the bathroom. A wretched, damaged face stares back at me. Amid the splatter of blood, I see multiple open lacerations and several broken front teeth. If Halloween were today, I'd have a truly scary mask.

I borrow a phone and call Carol to relate the incident. She's heartbroken and, voice quavering, sends her thoughts and prayers.

Having not accompanied me to Kampala, she cannot come now to comfort me.

I recall the phone number of Dr. Birungi, whom I know is also in Kampala on hospital business. I make the call and Dr. Birungi says he's on the way and will bring a surgical colleague.

I request that the U.S. embassy be informed of my injuries. Soon, a well-groomed Ugandan attaché, wearing a finely pressed suite, appears at my bedside. He opens a leather briefcase, embossed with an American eagle, and extracts a few forms.

"How can I help?" he politely asks.

"My money's been stolen; I will need some cash to pay for the emergency treatment," I lisp through smashed teeth.

"Are you in danger of immediate death?" is his odd response.

"What do you mean?"

"Will you be dead in twenty-four hours?"

"Geez, I hope not."

Replacing the forms, he snaps the briefcase closed. Smiling broadly, he suggests, "Stop by the embassy when you are better, and we will certainly assist." He hastily exits the emergency room.

Soon, Dr. Birungi and the surgeon arrive with appropriate suture material from the operating theater. After forty stitches are placed in my face, I am transported to a Catholic mission hospital that houses the only CT scanner in Uganda. After a few minutes in the tube, the X-ray tech requests that I interpret my own scan, as the radiologist will not arrive until morning. I appreciate the speed of self-service. I watch as slice after slice of my skull and brain appear on the monitor. Thankfully, there's no blood clot in the brain nor any skull fracture. Dr. Birungi pays the $180 bill for the ER services and CT scan. In the wee hours of the morning, I get a lift, via ambulance, to the mission guest house.

The next day, I greet the members of the Kellermann Foundation and particularly Dr. Jean Creasey. Jean is the Chairman of the

Board of the Kellermann Foundation. She's also my dentist. When I give Jean a broad toothless smile, all she can do is cry.

Carol and I discuss possibly returning to the United States. My resentment subsides enough for me to realize that the young medic was right; I am lucky not to be toe tagged and lying on a cold slab. If we leave Uganda, the thieves will have

Dr. Jean Creasey and
a battered Dr. Scott

deprived me of more than my money and possessions. They will have interrupted our work with the Batwa.

The only time I really notice my rearranged face is when I look in the mirror. As indoor lighting is poor, the repair looks reasonably presentable. I sport a mouthful of broken teeth, but I'm alive. My bar for gratitude has been reset; if I am not left for dead in a ditch, then I will choose to be joyful.

When I return to Kampala, I retrace the steps of my beating. I ask around and am able to locate the fellow who pulled me from the ditch. He comments, "Great to see you! I did not expect you to live." I profusely thank him for saving my life and present him with a gift certificate for a family meal at an upscale restaurant.

With a grin, he replies, "I will be searching the ditches more diligently."

My facial lacerations eventually heal, but the broken front teeth have to wait for dental care on our next trip to the States.

In an amusing twist of fate, immediately upon my arrival in the U.S., I'm scheduled to speak at the New York University School of Dentistry. Eating is difficult, enunciation is compromised, and more than a few dental students stare at me with the obvious intent of using their newly acquired skills. However, I do find a similarity between the NYU dental folks and the Batwa: neither dwell on the events of the past. The students ask what happened to my teeth, and when I tell them a bit about being beaten and left for dead, they respond, "Oh, we're sorry, but we are glad that you are alive." I agree with them that being alive is good, and they move on quickly, asking about life in sub-Saharan Africa and how they might use their skills and training in the service of others.

CHAPTER 28

✢ ✢ ✢

Partnering Against Tuberculosis

"Dogs do not actually prefer bones to meat,
it is just that no one ever gives them meat."

 • African Proverb •

When I return to Uganda, I especially look forward to reconnecting with my former rivals, the *abafumu*. If I had any doubts about my mission here, they are immediately dispelled by the *abafumu's* greetings.

At our first meeting, they search my face, curious for vestiges of the beating. With furrowed brows, several delicately touch the remaining scars on my face. I give them a wide smile and they are amazed at the restoration of my teeth. "Dr. Jean did a good job on my smile, didn't she?"

They seem delighted; however, several open their mouths wide or draw back their cheeks with a finger exposing a decayed or broken tooth while they garble, "When will Dr. Jean return?"

Reassuringly, they say, "Kampala is a dangerous place, we're happy you are here."

"You are safe here."

"You are one of us."

Being accepted and loved eases my anxiety. What an incredible gift.

Getting down to medical business, the *abafumu* express interest in my thoughts on *enkororo* (the cough or tuberculosis/TB). They become animated when I ask, "How do you treat TB?"

A heated discussion ensues: some advocate cutting, others spells and incantations, others an herbal approach. Finally, a venerable *omufumu* reluctantly states, "Our treatments for TB are not successful. We know that the disease is easily spread, so we try to avoid patients who have TB."

I explain our situation: "We have drugs to treat TB, but they must be taken daily for eight months. If a patient doesn't take the medicines as prescribed, there is a chance that they may develop drug-resistant TB. I'm as disheartened and frustrated as you. Only half of our patients complete the TB regimen."

We sit in silence.

After a long pause, my friend Batusa says, "Neither of us is treating this disease effectively. What if we combine our resources? By our working together, *omuswiija* is now not a problem. Can we do it again?"

As almost anything here can be a cause of celebration, we step outside for spirited singing, raising clouds of dust with vigorous dancing. Batusa kindly reminds me, "It doesn't matter how you dance, just that you are willing to try."

At the following meeting, medical students Sean Nelson and Jessica Duarte join us. Sean and Jessica have been looking forward to meeting the *abafumu* and have done their homework regarding TB. Speaking healer to healer, they explain the cause of TB and that it is spread by close contact. It is a common cause of death and has been increasing in Uganda.

The *abafumu* are shocked to learn that even the gorillas and monkeys can have TB.

Sean and Jessica show the *abafumu* charts, diagrams, and visual aids demonstrating how coughing transmits TB.

One *omufumu* breathes a sigh of relief, "I'm glad that TB is not spread by sex!"

Awkward laughter fills the room.

Questions come quickly, but Sean suggests that we head down to the hospital for a closer look at TB. At the hospital lab, as they had done with malaria, the *abafumu* gaze through microscopes while the lab techs instruct them to look for the stained red linear streaks in the sputum sample.

"Wow, there are a lot of them," one comments.

"Yep, that's a lot of TB," the lab tech responds.

They then don gowns and masks and accompany us to the TB isolation rooms. We view chest X-rays and talk with patients.

Sean and Jessica patiently explain the eight-month treatment regimen: "Four drugs taken for two months, and then two drugs for an additional six months. Almost all cases of TB can be cured by adhering to this regimen."

We return to the guest house for a bite to eat and then conclude our meeting, agreeing to meet again in a month. However, just before we depart, Sean asks the *abafumu* a question that should have been on my mind but wasn't. "Perhaps you have something to teach us about TB?"

Batusa, who has been fully engaged in our conversations, firmly states, "Yes, there is much that *bazungu* need to learn about TB. TB is a disease of poverty." Her voice rising, she accents, "Unless you understand poverty, you will never be successful in treating TB!"

Once again, I am humbled. My medical training has come face to face with the realities on the ground. Swathed in my science and armed with medical cures, I had not considered how my treatment proposals would fit into their day-to-day lives. My ignorance exposed, I freely admit, "I don't understand a life of poverty or the constraints of being poor—teach me."

Eye-opening comments ensue:

"*Bazungu* need to know how difficult life is in a remote village. Accessing health care usually requires a walk of many hours."

"Food is scarce and water supplies are distant."

"Many of us go to bed without eating. We worry that our children will not survive."

"We live day to day. We don't think about tomorrow."

"Those who have TB are poor and hungry. To successfully treat TB, the patients need to be fed."

I note, "We feed the TB patients for the first two-week phase of treatment while they are in the hospital."

"That is not enough. You need to provide food for the entire eight months of therapy."

Carol and I have a quick consultation. We realize that our budget is limited, but we tell the *abafumu*, "We value your suggestion; we will feed patients with TB for eight months."

Batusa then delivers the closer: "Dr. Scort, you misunderstand. Since TB is a disease of the poor, the whole family needs help. You must provide food for the entire family. And stop charging the TB patients for any treatment."

Carol and I gasp in unison. Carol is quicker to recover. She reassures me, "If the program is to be successful, we need to follow the *abafumu*'s advice."

I do quick mental math and realize that the cost of the feeding program pales in comparison with the monumental cost of treating patients who develop drug-resistant strains of TB from not regularly taking their medications.

I tell the *abafumu* that the decision is not mine and ask them to return in two weeks after I've discussed their solution with the management team.

The Bwindi Community Hospital's management team heartily endorses the plan and we scrape up the needed funds from our reserves. There will be no more charges for any TB care. Sputum testing for TB and hospital visits will be free. All patients with tuberculosis will be given food during their hospital stay. Five kilos of beans and five kilos of posho (cornmeal porridge) will be provided when they return biweekly for their outpatient supply of drugs. As an incentive, an *omufumu* will be offered a one-time allotment of five kilos of beans and five kilos of posho for each case of active tuberculosis they bring to the hospital.

When we gather two weeks later, the *abafumu* express their delight with the plan. I, too, am delighted. Not only is the medication being regularly administered, the patients and their families are receiving comfort, a sense of security, and relief from financial burdens. The cost by U.S. standards is trifling.

The *abafumu* take responsibility for their patients' completion of an unbroken, eight-month tuberculosis therapy regimen. The results are encouraging. There's a marked increase in the daily arrival of potential tuberculosis patients, many accompanied by the *abafumu*. Moreover, several patients who were chronically defaulting are now taking their medicines.

These traditional healers command considerable respect in the community. With their support, our TB efforts are far more effective. The *abafumu*'s community involvement and authority is priceless.

The *abafumu* and the hospital join hands, forming an organization named the Village Health Team (VHT). Membership grows to over five hundred. Each Village Health Team member oversees twenty to twenty-five households. They are on the lookout for cases of malnourished children, problem pregnancies, diarrheal diseases, and general community health issues. They also assist with immunizations. If a VHT member spots a problem, they use a toll-free, three-digit number to call an assigned BCH nurse for advice or to arrange a transfer.

The VHT members also visit TB patients in their home every few weeks and encourage compliance with the medications. The Bwindi Community Hospital's records confirm that over 96 percent of TB patients are now taking their medications regularly. The results of this collaboration are impressive; our program has the highest compliance rate for TB therapy in East Africa!

At a subsequent meeting, the *abafumu* ask that we assist with folks who are afflicted by mental illnesses. They relate that the traditional belief is that mental disease is caused by demons, but spells and incantations to dispel the demons are ineffective. They lament, "It saddens us that the villagers manacle the mentally ill person to a bed or chain them to a tree. There must be a better way." When we investigate, we find that most of these patients have a psychosis and will benefit from a long-acting, injectable anti-psychotic medication. Working with the Village Health Team members and our community mental health nurses, we provide the monthly injections. A few days after the first shot, they return with a hacksaw, unshackling these patients. The villagers are delighted.

A public health maxim called the "Inverse Care Law" states, "People most in need of medical care are the least likely to access it." This law applies to the developed as well as the developing world. The Batwa who need us the most are least likely to ask for help or even look for it. The Village Health Teams are the hospital's eyes, ears, and feet on the ground, bringing community health and healing to remote areas where health care had only been a dream.

Meeting with the Abafumu traditional healers

CHAPTER 29

✧ ✧ ✧

HIV and Peace

"When sleeping women wake, mountains move!"

━━• African Proverb •━━

The results of the TB and malaria interventions are outstanding. Nevertheless, there is one disease that we have not addressed, *sirumu*. *Sirumu* is translated as slim disease—HIV/AIDS.

When BCH staff meets with the Village Health Team to discuss HIV/AIDS, there is noticeable pushback. Knowing that the disease is transmitted by sex, they are extremely reluctant to discuss it openly. I tell them that even in the U.S., sex is a sensitive topic.

One Village Health Team member informs us that it is believed that if a man contracts *sirumu*, he can be cured by having sex with a virgin.

Another adds, "What about having relations with a Mutwa girl?"

This arouses Batusa's anger. She bursts out, "These practices are harmful! They do not work, and they should be stopped!!"

Another Village Health Team member asks, "I hear that you have treatments. Is that true?"

When a BCH nurse responds that effective drugs are available, there is a palpable sense of relief. The nurse adds, "The disease is never totally cured, so these medications require a lifetime of treatment."

I acknowledge that there is a stigma attached to HIV and suggest that the stigma and the resulting silence only increases the disease's spread. Reluctantly, members of the Village Health Team agree to discuss HIV.

I ask about their experiences with those infected with HIV.

One relates a story about a brother, "He develops *sirumu* and just becomes skin and bones."

Another states, "My sister has *sirumu*; her husband is dead. I am raising their four children. It is hard."

Other stories follow with the same ending.

"What can be done?" they ask.

Our nursing staff describes the drugs used to prevent and treat HIV. "But we are particularly interested in the prevention of mother-to-child transmission of HIV. If a mother has *sirumu*, and is not treated, then anywhere up to 45 percent of her offspring will develop *sirumu*. If an infant born with *sirumu* is not diagnosed and treated, then 50 percent will not live to their second birthday."

Many of the VHT members have seen young children succumb to this devastating illness. There is wholehearted agreement that children should be spared HIV. Buoyed up by the news they have received about the effectiveness of medications for HIV, the VHT members return to their villages to educate their residents. They identify those who are likely to have *sirumu* and bring them to BCH for diagnosis and treatment. They also encourage pregnant mothers to be tested for *sirumu*.

The results are nothing short of miraculous. We are delighted to discover that if the HIV positive pregnant mother is placed on highly active anti-HIV medication and if the child is given treatment from birth to one year, the transmission rate of HIV from mother to child drops to less than 1 percent. For the next two-year period, not a single infant contracts HIV. The feeling of success is heady. This is exactly the type of community self-care that we have been hoping to foster.

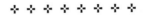

Peace Atwongyeire is an HIV counselor at the hospital. Peace has dark, smooth skin, a radiant smile, and a charming disposition. She has a deep spiritual center, attributing all to the joy of knowing Jesus. She's also HIV positive. Several years earlier, Carol and I came to know Peace from dining at her modest takeaway restaurant. The income from the restaurant supported her daughters and allowed her to complete an accounting course.

Early on a sultry summer day, Carol and I attend Peace's graduation. The entire school gives her a standing ovation when she is presented with her accounting diploma. We decide to top off her celebrations with a proposal.

As she returns to her seat, Carol asks, "How about coming to work at the BCH?"

"Wonderful! When do I start?"

"Today. We can give you a ride as soon as you pick up your belongings."

Carol and I talk briefly about the accounting work we'd like her to perform, but we also ask her, "Would you be willing to engage in work with the HIV community?"

Peace's energetic response surprises us. "Yes! This is what I know that God has called me to do. I've been hoping to find a way to reach out to others with HIV. This is perfect for me!"

Peace's broad, infectious smile and warm embrace becomes an inspiration to many at the hospital. Into an area of medicine that is fraught with stigma, isolation, and darkness, Peace breathes life and light.

Peace and Jean Creasey's lives become intertwined when Jean returns for another visit to the Bwindi. Like Peace, Jean has boundless energy. Jean's leadership of the Kellermann Foundation has been instrumental in the success of BCH; she has also assisted in establishing a dental unit. The hospital has the only dental chair in the district, serving a population of 250,000. Patients enter with distraught expressions and exit with their mouths clenched on a piece of blood-tinged gauze, which has been placed over the socket of their extracted tooth. Not an attractive sight at dental offices in the U.S., but here, the patients display broad, bloody smiles, filled with gratitude for services rendered and pain relieved.

While Jean's dental skills are appreciated, what the Ugandans love most is her breezy manner, exceptional ability to communicate, and willingness to engage on a deeply personal level. She's tireless.

Jean has gotten to know Peace during previous visits. They have developed a close bond. With the warmth of old friends, their greeting is punctuated by a long embrace.

At the following Sunday's church service, Peace presents a reflection on her life. She speaks with enthusiasm, but her talk is tinged with remorse: "At age 28, my husband died of AIDS. It was during a time when HIV was rampant, knowledge of prevention was scarce, and treatment was unavailable. I was devastated when I learned that I was pregnant and HIV positive. I was attempting to raise two girls on little income. We lived in a tiny house that needed repair."

Peace pauses and wipes a tear, "I was scared, lonely, and rejected. I am grateful to have survived." Then she shouts, "Today is my fiftieth birthday!"

The congregation rises as one and cheers. Led by the spirited choir, we sing a rousing song about redemption.

After the service, Peace requests that we come to her house and join in her birthday celebration. A large group of Peace's friends pack into her tiny living space. The windowless room is dimly lit by one bare bulb hanging from the ceiling. In sharp contrast, the blinding afternoon sun streams in through an open front door. Overflow guests perch on a bench outside. Two giant homemade and heavily frosted birthday cakes are cut and passed out on paper napkins. Eager hands reach out to share a portion of this rare treat.

Peace stands in the back of the room, a huge, glistening smile spreading ear to ear, making sure that every guest is offered a soda and slice of cake. Moving forward to speak to the whole group, she shares again her tale of gratitude: "I am HIV positive. In the late 1990s, it was believed that even shaking hands could spread the disease. I was like an Old Testament leper, untouchable, doomed to a short life. I lived on the fringe."

Peace's voice gains in determination.

"Now, over twenty years later, as part of the hospital staff, I help coordinate BCH's HIV program and outreach. We now test more than one thousand villagers per month. However, I am most proud of training HIV positive patients. They encourage people in their communities to be tested for HIV, and they demonstrate how to live successfully as an HIV-positive person."

Peace surprises me by directing her attention to me, saying, "Before Dr. Scott started the hospital, people with HIV walked three days to receive HIV treatment. Many could not do so and died. Now, we are not only surviving but also living joyful, fulfilling lives!"

Tears flow. Peace's open heart and her broad smile are contagious. She points toward a group of women sitting in a knot around a table, "Please welcome my friends who are members of the HIV Positive Women's Support Group. We meet regularly to encourage each other, and we have an income-generating project where we raise chickens and sell the eggs."

Beaming, Peace continues, "I would like to introduce these ladies to you."

One by one, each member of the support group stands and recounts their very personal and often tragic stories. Many of them had been forced to work as prostitutes to feed their children. They relate beautiful stories of deliverance, choosing to define the narrative of their lives not as victims, but as victors. The support from the women's group has changed their lives and has given them dignity.

Peace then introduces a young woman to Jean, "I told you that I was pregnant when my husband died from HIV. I learned then that I, too, was infected with HIV, but I had no access to therapy. This is my daughter from that pregnancy. Because she was born free from HIV, I named her Miracle."

Jean is stunned. She lets Peace know that the word "miracle" will have a new meaning for her.

The ladies rise in unison and sing with exuberance.

After the last song is sung, and the crowd disperses into the twilight, Jean and I walk back to the guest house overwhelmed from the events of the day. It is obvious that Jean is contemplating a weighty matter, so we pause along the way. "I had questioned the value of my efforts in the work I do for the Kellermann Foundation. Has it made a tangible difference? Should I persist in my efforts? However, as Peace finished her story, and the ladies closed with their theme song of living positively, those questions vanished forever."

She smiles at me, declaring, "I have known Peace, and that is enough!"

Miracle and Peace

CHAPTER 30

✧ ✧ ✧

The Weighty Issues of Poverty and Education

"Every morning in Africa, a gazelle wakes up.

It knows it must run faster than the fastest lion or it will be killed.

Every morning, a lion wakes up.

It knows it must outrun the slowest gazelle or it will starve to death.

It doesn't matter if you are the lion or the gazelle,
when the sun comes up, you'd better start running."

———• African Proverb • ———

Body weight is hard to maintain in Uganda. The Ugandan diet is neither appetizing nor nutritious. The staples are solely starches consisting of matoke, white rice, potatoes, and cassava. A thin sauce is added for flavor. Meat is a rarity. The only spice is salt. No Michelin Stars are going to be awarded to the local chefs. In addition to being bland and unpalatable, huge amounts of this fare must be ingested to maintain weight.

Attitudes regarding weight are vastly different between Uganda and the United States. Female obesity is highly prized in Uganda. Ugandan newspapers carry advertisements for formulas that encourage the reader to "Gain ten to twenty pounds and quickly find the man of your dreams." Carrying extra pounds is indicative of prosperity, a sedentary lifestyle, and a surplus of food. It also suggests that one is free from a wasting disease such as TB or HIV. One of the highest compliments one can give to a woman is, "Wow, you look great! You have gained weight!"

Carmel, a twenty-five-year-old Irish volunteer teacher, has arrived, eager to begin work. She's vivacious and healthy, and certainly not obese by western standards. Upon arriving at the primary school where we had arranged for her to teach, the headmaster proudly introduces her to the students at the morning assembly. He writes on the blackboard in large block letters, "WELCOME CARMEL, A FAT YOUNG WOMAN FROM AMERICA!" The students then loudly repeat in unison, "Welcome Carmel, a fat young woman from America!" Then they diligently copy the phrase into their workbooks.

The headmaster notices that Carmel is uncomfortable, not to mention beet red. He realizes his apparent indiscretion and hurriedly approaches Carmel and apologetically says, "Oh, I am so sorry for what I wrote. I didn't mean to embarrass you."

He promptly erases the blackboard and replaces it with, "WELCOME CARMEL, A FAT YOUNG WOMAN FROM IRELAND!"

The Bwindi Community Hospital children's unit deals with the other end of the nutritional spectrum: starvation. Although the Bwindi region is known for its incredible biodiversity, it has some of the highest rates of food insecurity reported worldwide. Two American pre-medical students, Mick and Tom Borecky, have come to assist with a poverty and nutrition survey. Mick and Tom are identical twins, almost indistinguishable from one another in intelligence, good looks, and cheerfulness.

We work together to compile a list of nutritional questions. One survey question initiates a lively discussion: "How many days in a week do you not have any food to eat?"

Mick is disbelieving. "There are people who go a whole day without eating?"

"Yes," I say, "Many folks do not have food for at least one day, but you need to reword the question. It should read, 'How many days in a week do you *and your family* have no food?'"

Mick and Tom are devastated. They have never heard of this level of food deprivation.

For the survey, we randomly select communities surrounding the Bwindi and interview the female heads of households. For the interview, each woman is paid $1.75, slightly higher than the daily wage, and she is given a soda and biscuit while we chat.

At one remote village, an hour's walk from the nearest road, Mick and Tom's cheerful disposition evaporates.

Mick laments, "I have interviewed families that are without food for two days per week."

Tom relates, "One woman says that her children don't cry from pain, they only cry from hunger." He continues, "One woman asked me, 'Do people in your country have food to eat EVERY day?' She was incredulous when I told her about refrigerators and how much spoiled food is discarded."

Mick adds, "Something needs to be done."

I ask them what they would propose.

They suggest, "Dealing with hunger and poverty will require a long-term solution, but in the short run, let's double the ladies' compensation!"

"Great idea! I'm sure they will gladly accept," I respond.

We return to the village and announce that the interview compensation has been increased to $3.50. The women erupt in cheers, embracing Mick and Tom, giving them hugs and pats on the back. It's hard to tell who is happier, the women or Mick and Tom.

On the ride home, we discuss hunger and its devastating effects. Tom paraphrases Gandhi, "There are people in the world so hungry that God cannot appear to them except in the form of bread."

I suggest that we visit the malnutrition ward at the BCH.

Mick and Tom with Batwa community members

The next day, Mick and Tom join the physicians as they make their rounds examining children in the malnutrition ward. This unit treats those in the late stages of starvation, either marasmus or kwashiorkor.

Marasmus is a condition that results from an insufficient intake of calories. A child with marasmus has the appearance of a wizened old man; wrinkled skin hangs loosely, the hair is thinned, deep sunken eyes peer from a bony frame. Conversely, Kwashiorkor is caused by insufficient protein consumption. The child develops a moon like face, protuberant belly, swollen legs, and reddish hair.

The therapy of malnutrition is straightforward: correct nutritional deficiencies and cure any underlying diseases. Although most of the cases of malnutrition are due to inadequate nutritional intake, all our children are screened for the nutrient-sapping diseases of parasites, bacterial infections, TB, and HIV. Often, simply increasing the amount of energy consumed (food) is all that is needed. Seven times daily, they are fed a simple formula of high-energy milk containing oil, sugar, and vitamins. As they easily shed body heat, we supply them with hats and sweaters.

On admission, the children typically don't interact with their environment. They sit quietly, not playing with other children, demonstrating very little emotion except irritability. They stare vacantly. The spark is gone.

A smile is the indicator that these children are improving. Our nursing staff will often break out into jubilant singing when a malnourished child flashes their first smile.

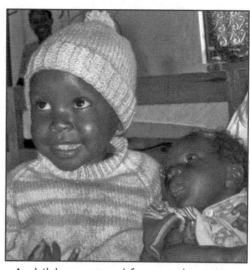

I explain to Mick and Tom, "The root cause of much of this malnutrition is a poverty of knowledge. These mothers have the land, the tools, and the

A child recovered from malnutrition

capacity to work; however, they don't know which foods are nutritious, how to best prepare them, and in what quantity."

"It's a matter of education?" they wonder.

In the center of the malnutrition unit, there is a kitchen. Here, the mothers are taught which foods are nutritious and how to prepare them. It's a far cry from the cooking shows on TV with modern ovens, microwaves, and colorful pots and pans, but it does the job nicely. Also, the cooks are less competitive. In their post-discharge home assessments, the Village Health Team finds most previously malnourished children are thriving, and so are their siblings.

I take Mick and Tom to a piece of land adjacent to our nutrition unit that most would consider unsuitable for planting. It's steep and rocky and the soil is poor. This land has been intentionally chosen as a demonstration garden to show that any piece of land, well-tended, can produce a bounty of crops adequate to sustain a family. The mothers of the malnourished children work in the garden. They are shown how to plant beans, maize, and vegetables. They learn what crops are needed to sustain their families.

The BCH also employs a cadre of agricultural workers who travel to distant villages by motorcycle, bicycle, or on foot, demonstrating planting techniques and providing information about nutritious crops.

I wish everyone could see our children's ward. Even though there are beds filled with sick and malnourished children, the ward is a joyful place. Every afternoon, drums are brought out and there is lively singing and dancing. Bed-bound kids slowly rise and either join in the dancing or clap to the rhythm. This Western doctor never imagined that the beating of drums could be so therapeutic.

The pediatric ward

Daily, tourists visit the hospital, usually fresh from trekking the mountain gorillas. They confess fears of seeing severely ill patients. I tell them that there is much to be experienced in sub-Saharan Africa, especially the remarkable flora and fauna. But for inspiration, there is little that compares to a visit to our children's ward.

When tourists enter the children's ward, they are surprised by its bright, welcoming atmosphere. Kids, with tubes dangling out of their noses or IVs suspended from their arms, take the visitors' hands and lead them around the ward, introducing the *bazungu* to the other kids.

At the rear of the children's ward is the fifteen-bed malnutrition unit. I lift an emaciated child from a bed, placing the child in the arms of one of the visitors.

"How old?" I am asked.

"Not sure, there are no birth records, I assume perhaps three to four years," I respond.

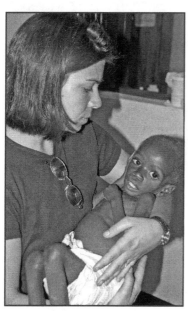

Rebecca and a child
with marasmus

As the tourist lifts the butterfly weighted child, a shocked look comes over their face.

The reaction is immediate: "How can this kid be so tiny? ...Why does such a degree of poverty still exist? ... My health and wealth are an embarrassment! ... What can I do to help?"

An encounter with these malnourished children is a first step in an awareness of the needs of much of the world. This awareness, combined with divine encouragement, will hopefully be a pathway to a deeper engagement with the needs of those less fortunate.

CHAPTER 31

✢ ✢ ✢

The Care of Mothers

"It takes a breast for a child to know its mother,
and it takes a mother for a child to know its father."

────• African Proverb •────

Bwindi Community Hospital

The Bwindi Community Hospital grows to 155 patient beds. For comparison, over half of rural hospitals in the U.S. have fewer than twenty-six beds. BCH is flourishing under an all-Ugandan staff and is recognized as one of the finest hospitals in East Africa.

From its inception, the main focus of the hospital has been maternal and child health. I have witnessed much grieving from a young child's death, but the death of a mother is devastating. Husbands insist that their wives bear many children, but they rarely assist with child rearing. Many times I have attempted to comfort a distraught husband as he hangs his head in sorrow. "What will my children do without their mother?"

Maternal health statistics for sub-Saharan Africa in general and Uganda in particular are shocking. In southwestern rural Uganda, statistics indicate that out of every 113 births, a pregnant mother will die. This is over fifty times the rate in the United States. The typical causes of death are infection, a child too large for the mother's pelvis and bleeding, coupled with a general lack of access to maternal care.

The good news is that the vast majority of these deaths can be prevented. The Bwindi Community Hospital has attempted to address this need by providing a maternity unit for normal deliveries, a well-equipped surgical theater where Cesarean sections can be performed, and public health outreach to the villages. Over the past several years, the hospital has worked closely with the traditional birth attendants and the Village Health Team members. We've taught them birthing techniques and encouraged timely referral of problem cases.

Our facility is in a remote location lacking any paved roads or public transportation. If a mother is laboring at home and has a complication, the arduous one- to two-day walk to our institution is not only painful, but potentially fatal. Mothers have requested a facility where they can reside at the latter stage of pregnancy. In response to their appeal, we construct a forty-bed Pregnant Mother's Hostel. Here, a bed, kitchen, and laundry facilities are provided. Education regarding childbirth, child rearing, and family planning is also offered.

The women tend to congregate in an open area behind the facility where they cook, wash clothes, and learn how to tailor. There is a true sense of camaraderie and joy. Delightful singing abounds.

The hostel is frequently exceeding capacity. Delivery rates at the hospital have increased from twenty deliveries per month in 2010 to around two hundred per month in 2017.

Through the provision of quality maternal health care, timely referral to the Bwindi Community Hospital, and access to the Pregnant Mothers' Hostel, the maternal death rate is reduced by more than 90 percent.

Our operating theater is equipped with appropriate supplies and a well-trained staff. Cesarean sections are an age-old surgery named after the Greek word *cesar*, which means to cut. Cesarean sections are the most satisfying of all surgical procedures. Through one incision, two lives are saved.

Referrals to the hospital are frequent and patients are commonly in dire straits. Our surgical team is well-trained and available at any hour. They take pride in being able to deliver a baby by emergency Cesarean section in less than twenty minutes, around half the time required in U.S. hospitals.

Transport of a pregnant woman in distress from a remote village is a remarkable event. She is typically borne on a stretcher constructed by woven reeds overlapping lateral poles. Bearers transport this makeshift ambulance at an amazing clip. Villagers run ahead, stationing themselves along the trail, waiting their turn at carrying. Even on the darkest night, without flashlights, these tag-team runners can convey a patient with incredible speed.

When I am told that a pregnant mother has arrived, members of the operating room staff join me, breathless from their sprint to the hospital. The mother is gently taken off the stretcher and placed on an examination cot. If it is determined that a rupture of her uterus is likely or that the infant's life is in imminent danger, the decision is made: "Let's operate!" Everyone springs into action. It is truly a joint effort with only one focus: healthy baby, healthy mother.

The patient is quickly transferred to the operating theater while the generator is started. The surgical theater's bright lights suddenly illuminate the room, an IV is inserted, an antiseptic solution doused on the abdomen, an apron thrown over my scrubs, gloves quickly donned, a scalpel placed in my hand, and … we pause. Together, we check through the possibility of complications, ask if adequate blood is on hand, and ensure that instruments are available should a more extensive procedure be required. At this point, I request that a member of the surgical team ask for God's guidance.

We inject the anesthetic ketamine. I make a swift, surgical incision, open the skin, and retract the muscles. Typically, in cases of imminent uterine rupture, I see the faint outlines of a child through the thinned uterine wall. As I open the uterus, the adage "make haste slowly" applies. This is the most precarious stage of the surgery;

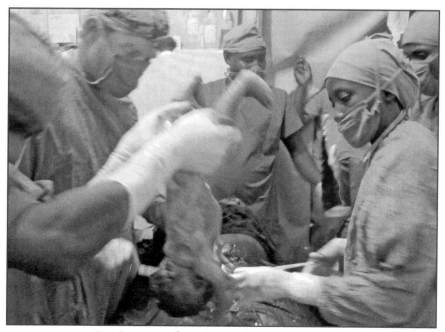

Dr. Scott preforming a Cesarean section

any excessive force can damage the uterine arteries, causing profuse bleeding. With a bit of gentle traction, out pops the infant with a cough and a cry. At the sound of new life, the entire operating crew breaks into spontaneous applause, jubilant singing, and, of course, dancing. The atmosphere of many delivery rooms in the U.S. would be much improved with applause, singing, and dancing.

After bleeding sites are clamped, we give thanks. Longer-acting anesthesia is administered, the abdomen is thoroughly cleaned, sterile drapes are applied, and my surgical gowns are exchanged for my apron. Then, the uterus, muscles, and skin are sutured closed, and the procedure is completed.

Late in the day on August 12, 2017, the surgical team is exhausted, having set a hospital record of twelve births, five delivered by Cesarean sections. We are pleased that mothers and infants are doing well. The midwives are tasked with handling the remaining laboring mothers. We retire to our guesthouse for a going away party for Danny, a volunteer medical student from England. The guesthouse manager, Daniel Jamison, assisted by his children Willow and Ansel, have prepared a fantastic meal. A goat and several chickens have been roasted, mounds of matoke are served, and lively music is blaring. It is a gala affair. We share good cheer and, of course, dancing.

We watch the sun set over the Bwindi Forest. Suddenly, a breathless midwife interrupts the gathering, "Please come quickly! There is an obstetrical patient who is close to death!"

I race to the obstetrical unit. When I arrive, the medical staff is focused on a semi-comatose pregnant woman who is covered in blood.

I join in the attempt to save her life.

The woman is pale, in shock from massive blood loss. She has no blood pressure and only a feeble pulse is perceptible. Her eyes are glazed over. She can only moan.

She is nameless.

We obtain a sketchy history from a "Good Samaritan" motorcycle driver who transported her to the hospital. He tells us that she was able to speak an hour earlier. "I find her collapsed on the forest's outer edge. I pick her and her son up from the side of the road, strap them on my motorcycle and bring them to you. Please save her life!"

I look up to ask him a few more questions, but he has disappeared.

We are aware that she needs blood immediately, but numerous attempts at inserting an IV are futile. Profound shock has collapsed her veins. We place her in a head-down position, and I focus on her barely perceptible jugular vein. Her life is in the balance. One stick — one chance for life. We ask for divine guidance and, thankfully, the catheter slides in effortlessly. A nurse stands at the bedside, hands squeezing a unit of blood, transfusing the life-saving liquid into her body.

She still has no blood pressure; her only hope for survival is for us to operate to stop the bleeding. We quickly transport her to the operating theater. Upon opening her abdomen, I see that her uterus has ruptured. Sadly, her infant has died much earlier. Her uterus continues to hemorrhage. No matter how many sutures I place or arteries I clamp, the bleeding persists. I make the difficult decision to remove the uterus, a procedure that I have rarely performed. These are the times that you must act and can only hope that your skills rise to the occasion. I begin the hysterectomy. After another hour, the uterus is removed, the bleeding is controlled, the blood pressure rises, and the patient stabilizes.

When I return to the guesthouse at midnight, I'm surprised by the sound of music. Danny's party is still in full swing. Everyone is elated that the woman has survived. We dance until the wee hours of the morning.

Later the next day, the patient regains consciousness. As I sit at her bedside, she recounts the harrowing story of her difficult, lonely trip, as she cradles her two-year-old son: "I am in labor but cannot deliver my child at home. I strap my son on my back and try to walk to the hospital. I hike all day through the forest, at night we sleep under a tree. In the morning, I can't stand. I am exhausted, and blood is pouring out of me. I realize that I am dying, and my young son will be an orphan. As I crawl, I pray that I make it to the hospital and that I can live. I am alone and hopeless. I cannot continue and I faint. Then I see bright lights, someone is sticking a needle in me, and I hear people praying for me."

With tears running down both our faces, I share in her joy as she declares, "I am grateful that my son has a mother to raise him and love him."

I ask her about the motorcycle fellow who brought her to the hospital, but she has no memory of a motorcycle ride. I inquire around the hospital and the community. No one knows him; he has simply vanished.

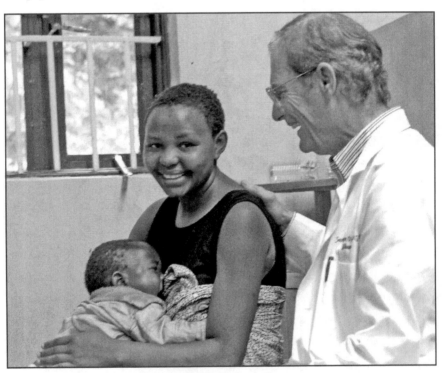

A smiling Victoria

PART V (2017 AND BEYOND)
For the Future

"Home is not where we live; home is where we belong."

—— • African Proverb • ——

CHAPTER 32

✣ ✣ ✣

From the Rainforest to the UN

"If you educate a man, you educate an individual,
but if you educate a woman, you educate a nation."

——— • African Proverb • ———

When we began our work in 2001, some Batwa had been settled on plots of land sprinkled around the Bwindi Forest. Initially, they were left to their own to construct dwellings for themselves. Since they moved so frequently in their rainforest life, these were small, temporary dwellings made of grass. From its inception, the Batwa Development Program has focused on enhancing life in the

Volunteers mudding a Batwa house

settlements by buying land, digging wells, adding permanent brick structures that can be used for spiritual gatherings or instruction in crafts or trades, and, perhaps most importantly, building improved homes for Batwa families. While we anticipate a day when the Batwa can have brick homes, by 2017, we have built some two hundred mud and wattle, tin-roofed homes. After the poles that support the house walls are erected and the corrugated tin sheets of the roof applied, the house needs "mudding," which amounts to stuffing slabs of mud, harvested by the Batwa from a nearby pits, between reeding that is secured on either side of the poles. The mud needs to be wet enough to be successfully pushed intact into crevasses—which means mudding the house gets everyone very muddy!

Over the years, most of these homes have been built with the help of donors from the U.S. or Europe. It is great fun! *Bazungu* work together with the Batwa digging in the mud pit, carrying mud to the appointed wall stuffers, and then throwing globs of it at the wall to cover any protruding sticks. Laughter abounds, and every-one encourages each other, especially the Batwa who cheer on the *bazungu*, even as they outwork them. Then, of course, afterward, everyone joins together in singing and dancing. Volunteers often tell us that mudding a Batwa house is the pinnacle of their visit to the Bwindi. Through laboring together, a home has been built and a deeper understanding between cultures has been forged.

Carol remembers the first house that we built for a Batwa family of four. As we toured the newly completed, four-room, 125-square-foot structure, Carol asked the family how many people could occupy this house. The husband calculated for a while and responded, "In a home this fine, at least twenty can live happily." Talk about high-den-sity housing!

Education is also a high priority for the BDP. Carol, with her teaching background, has fostered the educational system from seventy students in 2001 to 750 students in 2017, increasing to 1,500 in 2022. Three schools have been built and another renovated. A good example of such educational improvements is found at the Batwa settlement at Byumba. In 2001, the school there was a collapsing mud hut with thirty students. Now, 425 students study in Pres' Primary School, a sturdy facility, where a warm meal is provided daily.

The recently completed 450-student Kishanda School has a fully equipped computer lab. The children are flourishing. The Batwa elders tell us, "Our children are our future!"

Kishanda Community School

Some Batwa children have taken enthusiastically to school instruction, performing at a very high level. We first came to know a young Mutwa named Sylvia when we constructed a protected spring in her village. Sylvia was sitting with her mother and sister in front of their six-by-eight-foot thatched hut. The family's possessions were minimal, a few pots and pans, three threadbare straw mats with some tattered blankets. Sylvia was around eleven years old. She seemed bright and inquisitive but also quite shy and reserved. As we chatted with them, Carol asked Sylvia, "Are you happy?"

Sylvia emphatically responded, *"Ninyenda kwega omuishomero,"* (I want to study in school).

Sylvia's conviction inspired Carol and she agreed to support Sylvia's education. She could never have foreseen all that would come from sponsoring Sylvia.

Sylvia faced some formidable challenges along the way. While in high school, she met an older man and became pregnant. The man already had a family and abandoned Sylvia. She was devastated and left school, running away to a distant town. BDP staff member Levi Busingye located her, convinced her to return home, and encouraged her to consider continuing education while her mother raised her child. While the arrangement worked, Sylvia lacked the drive she had earlier displayed. At that crucial time in her life, Sylvia received motivation and encouragement from two women from our hometown in California.

On a rainy June day, Dr. Jean Creasey and Dr. Sarah Woerner arrive at the Bwindi. Sarah is a pediatrician who has come to BCH to teach a course in neonatal resuscitation to the maternity staff. Sarah is always surrounded by children; the kid in her is an irresistible magnet for the youngsters.

Dr. Sarah Woerner with Batwa children

Over the years, through their frequent visits, Jean and Sarah have been mentors to young women, providing inspiration and counsel to those who waver in their commitment to their futures. Both have known Sylvia for years and recognize that Sylvia's inner spark requires encouragement.

Relaxing over a cup of tea at the guesthouse, Jean and Sarah have a lively chat with Sylvia. Jean and Sarah describe the decisions and sacrifices they have made as they balance their careers with their duties and commitments as mothers and wives. They encourage Sylvia, telling her, "God has given you many gifts: intelligence, determination, and a heart for your people. And, the best of all, you are a woman with a purpose!"

They ask her, "How will you use your gifts?"

Sylvia only gazes away, disinterested.

After a rather uncomfortable silence, Jean reflects on her personal trials, "Sylvia, I went to dental school after giving birth to my third child. I had to think long and hard about school. I decided to stick with my studies. I found out how tough I was."

Jean asks Sylvia, "Are you tough?"

This question resonates with Sylvia, and she brightens. "Yes, I am tough!"

Jean encourages her, "Well, use your toughness to succeed in life." Sylvia is emboldened by Jean's advice. When she discusses her situation with her Batwa friends, they also encourage her to continue her studies: "We want you to lead us." Sylvia repeats her senior

Dr. Jean Creasey and Sylvia

year of high school, excelling in her studies. From high school, she moves on to university and becomes one of the first Batwa to graduate from university.

After graduation, Sylvia returns to the Bwindi to work with the BDP. Life has come full circle for Sylvia. She's now giving back to the Batwa, grateful for the opportunity she has been given, and she's inspiring them.

A few months later, Sylvia finds herself in New York City. Our son Josh and his wife Lara, who live in New York, show her the sights. She rides in a crowded subway, eats her first pizza, and, at the end of the tour, visits the Empire State Building. Sylvia is intimidated when she gazes up, "We are going to the top? How will we get there?"

"It will be fun," Josh assures her.

The friendly elevator ticket vendor cheerfully inquires of the three, "Where are you from and what do you do?"

Josh: "We live in Brooklyn. I am an attorney in Manhattan."

"Okay."

Lara: "I am a professor at Cornell."

"Okay."

Sylvia: "I am a Batwa pygmy from Uganda."

The ticket vendor seems surprised but continues, "And what are you doing in our fair city of New York, little lady?"

With a broad grin, Sylvia responds, "I've been invited to speak at the United Nations regarding enhancing indigenous peoples' rights."

"Oh my goodness! You are carrying a lot on your shoulders."

Despite the intimidating environment and august assembly at the UN, Sylvia is poised as she describes the plight of the Batwa and details their current efforts toward gaining personal independence and dignity.

Upon Sylvia's return to Uganda, she accepts an invitation to address the Ugandan parliament about the challenges that the Batwa face. She also decides to pursue her education even further, becoming the very first Matwa to obtain a master's degree.

Sylvia

When we initially came to live in Uganda, it seemed to us that one of our special callings was to be the "voice of the voiceless." Now, thanks especially to the work of the BDP, the Batwa have found spokespeople from among their own. As head of the education wing of the BDP, Sylvia speaks both for and to her people. She advocates for their right to access education and healthcare, their right to live in peace with their neighbors, and their right to dignity and respect as men and women made in the image of God. As others like Sylvia arise from among the Batwa, there is reason to hope that this oppressed people will speak to their neighbors and to the larger world, reminding them that no people should be ignored and forgotten as the Batwa once were.

CHAPTER 33

✤ ✤ ✤

The Birth of a Nursing School

*"If we stand tall, it's because we are standing
on the shoulders of many ancestors."*

———— • African Proverb • ————

first met Jim Jameson and Steve Wolf at an upscale safari lodge close to the official entrance to the Bwindi rainforest. This lodge is a place that I often visit: the beverages are cold, and the hospitality is warm.

A table over, I overhear Jim and Steve's excited talk about a visit with the gorillas. Thrown in are snippets of another adventure that piques my interest: "Mongolia … fly fishing … huge trout … Russian helicopter." I love to fly fish and feel a kindred bond with anyone else who loves the sport. I introduce myself and they admit me into their conversation. Their description of flyfishing Mongolia is vivid: the thump, thump, thump of the helicopter rotors hovering over pristine waters; "Look at the size of that monster! Put her down!"; the zing of the fly line as it pays out attached to a high-flying trout; the high fives after a successful netting.

At some point, Steve turns to me and asks, "Are you the one who is involved with the hospital that we visited this afternoon?" I confirm these suspicions and receive a further request, "Please join us at dinner. Your nurse, Jane Anyango, who took us on the hospital tour will also dine with us."

At dinner, Jane is delightful company. She is intelligent, has a brilliant smile, and is very convincing. While I am downing a delicious steak, Steve asks about the hospital's needs.

Sensing that these two might consider donating, I rack my brain, attempting to recall our ten-year strategic plan:

"Number one is expanding our medical ward."

"Not interested."

"Okay, then how about improving our surgical suite?"

"No, not interested."

"Our X-ray is aging."

"No interest in X-ray."

At this impasse, Jane comes to my rescue and suggests, "How about a nursing school?"

Jim and Steve's eyes light up.

Jane continues, "It will be the only school of its kind, serving a population of over one million. Our school will train the people living in our region and concentrate on preventing illnesses."

The thought of training nurses who focus on public health and the prevention of disease is exciting to them. There is enthusiasm all around the table. I share their eagerness, but what about the money? We're talking big bucks.

As if on cue, Steve asks, "How much would a nursing school cost to build?"

Reaching for the moon, but willing to take anything, I say "$150,000 would probably suffice."

"We're in!"

I am flabbergasted and thank them profusely. I caution that the final decision regarding embarking on nursing education must be made by the hospital management committee.

The following day, I discuss the possibility with BCH's management. They are very encouraging. Robert, the head of nursing, notes that we could employ the best and the brightest of the nursing school's graduates at BCH. Dr. Birungi adds, "The hospital can provide administrative, accounting, and human resources support, and our doctors can teach at the school."

The management committee suggests that we get firm figures regarding cost. "$150,000 might be a bit low."

When we take the time to run the cost analysis for construction, it becomes obvious that my initial projection is way off. I email Steve and Jim and suggest a more realistic figure: "It appears like it'll be closer to $300,000."

A day later, I receive their response, "Okay, but we need well-defined estimates."

We continue our discussions with engineers and builders. I send another email: "It looks closer to $500,000."

Several days pass before they reply, "Okay, we're still in, but we need exact numbers."

After we do an exhaustive review of all the contingencies, my next email is even more painful. "The final estimate is $650,000."

We wait anxiously, this time even longer, but then the reply comes back: "We're in. Let's go ahead."

We turn to our friend, Simi Lyss, for his graphic design skills. Construction begins as soon as plans are approved. Jane heads the school, while Jerry Hall partners with Rotary International to provide the school's necessary equipment and supplies.

Through this collaboration, The Uganda Nursing School-Bwindi (UNSB) emerges on a sixteen-acre plot of land that has lain fallow for years. It's within easy walking distance of the hospital. Rather than send large textbooks from the U.S., we incorporate medical and nursing texts into Kindles. Classrooms are equipped with smart boards. Several U.S. nursing schools collaborate in advising us how to set up our nursing program and the provision of distance teaching.

We plan on admitting a class of twenty-four students per year with a three-year course of study. A total of seventy-two students

Uganda Nursing School Bwindi

will be housed at the school. However, over the next several years, UNSB grows to over four hundred students! A scholarship program provides tuition for needy students, but most are able to pay. By 2018, UNSB is practically self-sufficient. Jim and Steve's vision has become a full-blown reality.

The school serves a variety of purposes. First, since Jane and her faculty and staff are exacting and thorough, UNSB produces high-quality nurses for Bwindi Community Hospital. Moreover, BCH's doctors and experienced nurses prove to be capable instructors; many enjoy working with the nursing students, and the instruction also sharpens their skills. Perhaps the greatest benefit is what the nursing school provides for this remote area: a place for good students to continue their education, which, in turn, will lead to employment, many in their home area.

Instead of gravitating to the cities after their studies, as is the case of many Ugandan graduates, the UNSB students are committed to utilizing their talents and skills in their rural home areas. In the process, their families and communities will be enriched.

UNSB prepares its students well; each year close to 100 percent of its graduating nurses pass the certification exam. This excellent performance record has attracted students from other regions and other tribes besides the Bakiga and Batwa. This result is a kind of cultural diversity, as students from different tribes enjoy sharing their traditional dances and stories. Combined with the hospital, the nursing school has not only lifted up the Bwindi region by providing good quality healthcare, but it has also become a hub of cultural, social, and economic opportunities for the many residents who live in the rural communities surrounding it.

The nursing school is located less than a kilometer from the towering ficus tree where Carol and I first held our mobile clinic. My heart is both uplifted and humbled to think of the difference I now see. The people we met there were some of the poorest in Africa; medicine was almost non-existent. In less than twenty years, patients are now welcomed and cared for at a bustling hospital, babies are born healthy, mothers survive and thrive, and a new generation is being trained in providing the best possible healthcare with love and concern—as the motto of Uganda Nursing School Bwindi states, "Excellence with Compassion." With recent approval to transition to a full university which will be named African University of Science and Management (AUSM), the school will have a new level of excellence to achieve—being truly awesome.

The poor remain with us in this remote and forgotten part of the world, and the need is everywhere, but God and his faithful people have established a foothold. A next generation can begin their good work from here.

CHAPTER 34

✜ ✜ ✜

Going Home

*"Return to old watering holes for more than water;
friends and dreams are there to meet you."*

———— • African Proverb • ————

"I am because we are."

———— • African Proverb • ————

Over the last several years, it is apparent that Carol's and my advice is less needed and, I must admit, less heeded when given. I find I do not mind so much. Dr. Birungi is heading the hospital with extraordinary competence and integrity; Robert Kamugisha, who has taken over for Jane while she pursues further study in the U.S., is guiding the nursing school with a steady hand; the BDP has excellent leadership from Rev. Bernard, Rev. Jovahn, his wife Penelope, and Miracle, Peace's daughter. Bishop Dan Zoreka, who replaced Bishop John in 2010, enthusiastically supports our work and shepherds the Anglican diocese we serve with vision and Christian care.

Carol and I are in regular email communication with Simi and Jerry, and they have been encouraging us to make a gradual withdrawal from the daily operations of the hospital. I am becoming increasingly aware that it's time to return to the States, but I'm reluctant to go. I have a deep sadness when I consider releasing the attachments that I have to the Bwindi and the Batwa.

Carol questions my motives: "Are you defined by the hospital? Are you having trouble relinquishing power? Remember what Simi told you, 'This project will never be independent and sustainable if you remain at its center.'"

I lament, "It's difficult for me to consider leaving this all behind. It's part of who I am."

She responds, "The Ugandans need to make their own decisions. They are the future."

Trying to make light of the situation, I note, "Some decisions that I have made were real doozies ... but they made for great stories."

Carol reminds me, "You were wondering why the hospital management has been scheduling meetings when you were occupied in surgery. Could they be sending you a message?" More seriously she adds, "And, our grandkids need grandparents."

After BCH's morning gathering, Carol and I meet a group of newly arrived U.S. medical students.

I smile when they tell me, "We have never sung or danced at our medical staff meetings. These meetings are a lot more fun!"

When the students ask me how this hospital was started, I suggest that we take a short walk. Along the way, I explain that a little over a decade ago, the Batwa's only access to medical care was through our mobile outreach clinics. Carol recalls our aging Land Rover groaning on impossibly steep and narrow roads as we delivered medical care to places where it had never been available.

On a rise overlooking the hospital, we stop at a stately ficus tree. I tell them that this is where it all began, here and under other ficus trees around the park. Their eyes widen as Carol describes, "Hundreds of patients fanned out around this tree." Carol smiles, "The best part was the music. We were constantly serenaded by drumming and singing."

I point to a flat area nearby. "This is where we laid woven mats where I assisted students like you in performing open-air surgeries. Over there, Carol cleaned out tropical ulcers."

We walk to the base of the tree. "And, in this shade lay kids with severe malaria. Do you see those hanging vines? That's where we attached their IVs."

Pointing towards the hospital, almost embarrassed by the pride I feel, I tell them, "From medicine practiced under this ficus tree we have built a fine facility, supported by a cast of well-trained and compassionate staff. Ugandans are now doing the work. They are the mentors and teachers. They, not *bazungu*, are the future of health care in this region."

Carol says, "Thanks to many people's efforts, the tiny seed of care that we planted under this ficus is now bearing fruit!"

I admit to the students, "It has been tough for me to step back from the management and clinical duties. I love it here."

Wrapping her arm around my waist, Carol tells the students, "The Bwindi will always be in our hearts, but our lives can move on. We do not have to always be here to steer what we were so privileged to begin. Our God is bigger than that."

She gently whispers, "Honey, it's time for us to go home."

It is good to be back in beautiful Northern California, amongst friends and family, while my Ugandan friends competently manage the hospital and nursing school. I throw my hat back into the ring of medical care in the region of Nevada City; while it is a different kind of work, it is important to do. Medicine, after all, is a calling. If I have the strength and desire to provide it—and the skill—I should.

Coming full circle, Diane Stanton, the very person who first inspired Carol and me to go to Uganda, has taken over as Executive Director of the Kellermann Foundation at its headquarters in Dallas.

Diane's love for the Batwa runs deeper than anyone I know. Her constancy as their helper and defender now spans almost thirty years. Diane and I consult often as we stay abreast of developments in the three wings of the foundation's work: the BDP, the hospital, and the nursing school. Also, when the KF Board gathers, I try to be there.

In time, I begin traveling again to the Bwindi. Carol comes less often, although we do have a special trip together when we bring our grandchildren. Daniel Jamison maintains our little house next to the rainforest; it comes to be part of a complex of guesthouses called the "gorilla houses"—named for the gorillas who occasionally visit.

In 2019, I am honored to be awarded a Fulbright Scholarship to teach global health/tropical medicine at our Uganda Nursing School Bwindi. My first day of class, I stand before ninety bright-eyed nursing students, all wearing well-pressed uniforms, Kindles in hand, watching my every move.

I begin my lecture by asking the students, "What qualities define a great nurse?"

"Compassion," one shouts.

"Knowledge of disease," from another.

"Skill administering medicine."

Not a bad start.

I then ask them, "What do you consider to be the difference between a nurse and a doctor?" as I proudly point to "Scott Kellermann, MD" emblazoned on my white medical jacket.

"A doctor prescribes medicine, and a nurse administers it."

"A doctor performs surgery and the nurse assists."

A young female student rises and makes a statement that rocks me: "A doctor treats the disease, but a nurse attends to the whole patient."

Painful but true! These students are perceptive and grasp the need to provide holistic health care. I tell them, "Let's learn together."

For my days off from teaching, I continue my habit of visiting Batwa villages to maintain my language skills. I park my motorcycle at the beginning of a narrow trail that leads to a small village of huts overlooking the Bwindi. I spend several hours in the village talking with the Batwa, especially the children.

From a Western perspective, these visits aren't productive. However, there is an expression that the Batwa are prone to tell me when I get too busy: "*Abazungu nokujwara eshaaha, kwonka abafrica baine obwire,*" (Westerners wear watches, but Africans have the time). Through most of my life in medical school and practice, I've been goal oriented and living in time segments. These Batwa have taught me the value of taking the time to develop deeper relationships.

When I arrive at the Batwa village, I'm invited to rest and talk. I always bring a bit of food and we eat together. They have proven to me that food is more delicious when shared. The kids tend to be very animated. They ask many questions, are patient with my answers, and correct me with humor when I routinely stumble with pronunciations.

I gaze across toward a ficus tree. Under this tree, a decade earlier, lay seriously ill children, receiving life-saving care.

As we sit, all squeezed together, elders, women, and children, I casually ask the Batwa what they appreciate most about the projects that we have engaged in over the years. "Is it the land we've helped you acquire, the access to a good medical facility, education for your children, clean water/sanitation, or homes constructed?"

I'm moved by their response: "*Kumara Obwire.*" *Kumara Obwire* loosely translates to "just hanging out." They explain, "It's the relationship with you that we value more than all the projects."

Another adds, "It's through our working together that the projects are successful."

An elder, who has been listening intently, says, "We have an expression, *Agari hamwe nigo gaata eigufa,* (It takes all the teeth to break the bone). It's a powerful force when people are united and work together for a common cause."

An elderly woman comments, "We love that you and Carol live with us and bring your friends to assist.

Another confirms, "*Turya Batwa*," (We are all Batwa).

Kids hold my hand and sing as I return to my motorcycle. I am abundantly aware that I've received much more than I have ever given. It is true that I have helped bring medical care to a group of people verging on extinction. With support from around the globe, I've helped build a hospital, a nursing school, and educational facilities for Batwa children. But, oh, what I've learned in return! The value

Dr. Scott sitting with Batwa children

of relationships. The importance of love and friendship. The freedom that comes from living a life without a watch to dominate it. The necessity of respect for the environment and the need to live within it without destroying it. The understanding that true wealth comes not from untold abundance and the accumulation of stuff, but from small things like the sharing of food, dancing, and friendship.

Albert Schweitzer said, "I don't know what your destiny will be, but one thing that I do know: the only ones among you who will be truly happy are those who have sought and found how to serve."

Carol and I are luckier than most people. We have been given this great opportunity to live with the Batwa and serve those less fortunate in a fascinating area of Africa. We have learned much about the Batwa, and even more about ourselves. Our relationship as a couple is all the richer for it. Medicine practiced under a healing tree in the remote Bwindi has restored my soul—a true gift.

Acknowledgements

✤ ✤ ✤

"Be sure to entertain strangers.
For thereby some have entertained angels unawares."

—— • Hebrews 13: • ——

Carol is the wind under my wings who continues to lift me up when I fall, dries my tears, and provides encouragement and love—thank you Carol! Working in Africa has offered many opportunities for encountering "angels in disguise," arriving at auspicious moments. Holy Trinity Church, Christopher Seal, and Tom Ewert believed in our work. Don Fultz, a consummate Rotarian, taught me the gift of building relationships and the art of raising money, all done with joy. Steve "Blackie" Gonsalves' wide smile and joy of life was an incredible uplift. Dick Panzica is owed a debt of gratitude for starting the Kellermann Foundation. To Simi Lyss, thanks for your friendship and mentoring. My thanks to Jerry and Tasha Hall for providing strategic planning, assuring sustainability of the institution, and being my friends.

The work with the Batwa pygmies began with Diane Stanton. Diane lighted the flame by her generous heart for those less fortunate, and Laura Corley has continued this tradition. My thanks to Sally Stillings for providing much needed organizational skills not only for the Kellermann Foundation but also for my life. Julia Amaral and Mark Strate have been a treasured resource for friendship and advice for decades; another book could be written about your engagement at the Bwindi. Dave and Gayle Porter, your encouragement and spiritual uplift are cherished. Emily Spitzer, you visited Uganda, saw the need, and built Kishanda School, giving the youth the gift of education. Jim Jamison and Steve Wolf, thanks for your support, counsel, and the provision of quality nursing education. Dr. Sarah Woerner, I have learned much from your friendship, encouragement, and willingness to whole-heartedly engage life. I had known Dr. Jean Creasey for many years but came to truly appreciate Jean when she was chairperson of our board. Her insights into a life fully lived, by loving boldly and forgiving freely, continues to be inspirational. This manuscript would have lain fallow if it were not for the encouragement of Stacy Lippert. Stacy's literacy skills, support, and friendship were the catalyst for this book coming to life. To the edits of John Sloan, whose advice and friendship helped produce a readable work. Daniel, Rachel, Willow, Ansel, Saayuuni Jamison—thanks for continuing the ministry at the Bwindi.

I appreciate the support from the Fulbright Scholars Program. For the first time in fifteen years, I was paid to do what I love—thanks! As a Fulbright Scholar, I was encouraged to teach, undertake a research project, and given time to organize my musings into book form.

To Bakersfield, Calvary Bible Church, Richard, Gerald, Mark, and "Just" Jack, thanks for building Pres' School and for your inspiration.

Lillian Niwagaba, thanks for your friendship and for patiently correcting my Rukiga. Andy, Diane, and Lauren Chang, thanks for your years of support and encouragement. Gage McKinney, you believed in me and motivated me to write. Paul Douville, thanks for the good times shared and your humor. Craig Kellermann, we have walked many a road together and remain not only brothers but continue with a deep abiding love. Granddaughters Lena, Sarah, Clara, Ella, and Mays, it's an honor to be your granddad. Thanks to Ivens Robinson, who organized a bicycle project for the women of the Bwindi and whose historical and literary perspective rocks.

Much of the inspiration for improvements to this manuscript is due to edits and insights from my friend Dr. Charlie Pinches. Thanks, Charlie, for your sage advice and thoughts about the spiritual virtues.

I am most thankful for the litany of friends at the Bwindi who taught me their language, customs, and traditions but, more importantly, welcomed a *muzungu* into their culture with a hospitality that was beyond what I could comprehend. Thanks for the good times, the close friendships, and best of all, the laughter: Richard Magazi, Levi Busingyi, Chief Elphaz, Enos Komunda, Dr. Birungi Mutahunga, Dr. Leonard Tutaryebwa, Dr. Ricky Baryuhanga, and Batusa. Knowing you all has made me a better person.

About the Author

❖ ❖ ❖

Mamia and Dr. Scott

Scott Kellermann, MD, is a graduate of Tulane School of Medicine where he also received his Master's in Public Health and Tropical Medicine. He currently serves as an Adjunct Professor at Tulane School of Public Health and Tropical Medicine and is an Assistant Professor at California Northstate University College of Medicine. He has published articles in professional journals of medicine on such topics as the Zika and monkey pox viruses, and on public health in Africa, especially in the Bwindi region of Uganda where he founded

Bwindi Community Hospital. He is the recipient of several awards and distinctions such as Rotary International's "Service Above Self" award (2013), the Dalai Lama's "Unsung Heroes of Compassion" (2014), Tulane School of Public Health's Alumnus of the Year (2016), the Fulbright Scholar award (2018), the AMA's Nathan Davis Award for International Service (2018).

Scott lives with his wife Carol in Nevada City, California, where they have received the support of friends and associates through their more than twenty years of service in southwest Uganda, as this book chronicles. They have two children and five grandchildren, all of whom have participated in different ways in this work of care and compassion. Scott returns to Uganda often to practice medicine at Bwindi Community Hospital, lecture at Uganda Nursing School Bwindi, visit his many friends from the Batwa tribe, and encourage his Ugandan colleagues as they continue to serve and heal.

Made in the USA
Middletown, DE
21 August 2024

59549000R00144